The Goodbye Year

To Ann,
A mother of
my heart. The
Best is yet to come.
Really !! :)

Jeni

The Goodbye Year

wisdom and culinary therapy
to survive your child's
senior year of high school
(and reclaim the *you* of you)

a month-by-month guide with recipes

Toni Piccinini

The Goodbye Year
Seal Press
Copyright © 2013 Toni Piccinini
Published by
Seal Press
A Member of the Perseus Books Group
1700 Fourth Street
Berkeley, California
www.sealpress.com

Library of Congress Cataloging-in-Publication Data

Piccinini, Toni
The goodbye year : surviving your child's senior year in high school / by Toni Piccinini.
pages cm
ISBN 978-1-58005-486-7
1. Mothers. 2. Mother and child. 3. High school students. 4. Loss (Psychology) I. Title.
HQ759.P5225 2013
306.874'3—dc23
2013016149

9 8 7 6 5 4 3 2 1

Cover design by Gopa & Ted2
Interior design by Gopa & Ted2
Printed in the United States of America
Distributed by Publishers Group West

For my mother and my daughter, and all moms past, present, and yet to be.

♡

There is nothing else like motherhood on this side of heaven. I am so grateful to be included in this club.

Author's Note

This is a work of nonfiction. Conversations and events are represented to the best of my memory. To ensure the privacy of my fellow moms and the "ladies" in my cooking classes, I have changed their names, their physical characteristics, and the number and gender of their children. Though I'm sure you know who you are. I'll let you decide if you want to tell.

Contents

INTRODUCTION:

Ignorance Is Bliss

•••

THE SUMMER BEFORE, 2004
RECIPE: *Torta della Stagione*

The sweet dough relaxed under the heel of my hand and settled into the form of a rustic rectangle. In the glass bowl on the counter, the sliced peaches helplessly surrendered their juice, releasing their natural tang into the mix of amaretto and sugar. An afternoon breeze, cooled by the coastal fog, gave a tease of freshness to a kitchen warmed by the day and the heat of the oven. I placed the peach slices, now slippery like baby golden fishes, onto the dough in a herringbone pattern and crimped up the edges, leaving the imprint of my fingers, a part of me. My mind and senses were totally engaged with my culinary endeavor; I was an easy target. My French lover approached as stealthily as a hairless cat, and as he pressed the length of himself against me, he found the spot below my left ear with his practiced tongue and whispered . . .

Okay, the peaches and the dough were real and it was freaking hot. But that summer I was wont to imagine a "what if" life. Just for fun, of course, because, I mean, come on, I had the perfect life: hubby Jeff; three kids, Page (sixteen going on seventeen, just like *The Sound of Music*), Ross (thirteen), and Banks (twelve); Indy the dog, well past adolescence but not an old man; and our eighty-two-year-old cottage in the burbs of Marin County, California. It's just that it was summer, the season of daydreaming. Right? Wrong. The siren song of my imagination was really more like a muted shriek from Cassandra, trying to give me a place to escape to and hide from the reality that was crashing down. In a few short weeks, my firstborn and only daughter was going to start her senior year of high school. For the next eleven months, every occasion our family celebrated, from the World Series to Groundhog Day, would be The Last Time!

A huge ending was coming to a life near me, and I wasn't ready.

You're not ready either, Mom. Your child's senior year of high school will achingly drag on even as it flies by at warp speed. You will watch your seventeen-year-old act like a two-year-old one day and comport himself like an officer and a gentleman the next. You will be treated to three-dimensional Technicolor memories of your young motherhood and then catch a passing glimpse of yourself in the mirror and wonder who in the hell is staring back at you.

The summer before Page's senior year, I was pretending that my life was just fine, like it was just swimming along the way it had been since I took on the welcomed role of mother. I was oblivious to who I was and who I had become. It is easy to forget yourself. It is so busy being a mom. It fills up your days and allows you to live a life of triage, which keeps you spinning in place. You function on a "need to do it now" basis. The most emergent tasks get priority, even if those tasks are mundane. Field trip permission slip needs signing, don't forget to buy the

It is so busy being a mom. It fills up your days and allows you to live a life of triage, which keeps you spinning in place. You can make lists and check things off, and one day tumbles into the next until finally you realize that this—your motherhood as you know it—is ending. If you allow it to penetrate, that realization comes to you at the beginning of your child's senior year of high school.

cloves for the art project, don't we have some foam core left over from last year's Miwok poster? You can make lists and check things off, and one day tumbles into the next until finally you realize that this—your motherhood as you know it—is ending. If you allow it to penetrate, that realization comes to you at the beginning of your child's senior year of high school.

I enjoyed three Goodbye Years, and they couldn't have been more different from one another. I was a different person each time, too. But Page's senior year was the watershed. Everything that came after led me down the path of discovery of who I am, and that started with the painful acknowledgment that I was coming to the end of the most important chapter in my life. Being a mom. Or so I thought.

August 2004

I am folding Page's laundry and I am weeping. Not a full sob, more of a tear-leaking, shaggy-breathing cry that in the past few months has come to be a frequent occurrence.

Jeff walks by, notices, and asks, "What's a matter?" How can he not know? It is the beginning of her senior year of high school.

"This is just so terrible," I say as I fold her panties in thirds, making another small packet to add to the stack of her clothes that I have smoothed and folded with absurd precision. "It's all coming to an end."

"Because she is going to college next year?"

"Yes," I say. Of course. Terrible. Our family of five is ending. It's over.

"Honey, you need to get out of the laundry room."

I have observed that what I think about comes to me. Whether I am thinking of something lovely (an old friend whom I haven't heard from in a while calls me the very day she is in my thoughts) or something troubling (worrying that I'm going to be late if there is traffic on the beautiful yet busy Golden Gate Bridge), if I think about it enough, it will arrive. And when we think about something all the time, we can't help but talk about it to our friends, which leads to more talking about it, and then later more thinking about what we have just talked about.

During my first Goodbye Year, I was constantly thinking and talking about the changes our family would experience when Page left for college. I created space for a terrific void, and I would find myself there, helpless against the pull of that dark

There is something about senior year that

forces us to recognize the truth: Even though we

may have spent twenty years perfecting the idea

that we are steering the life of another, it is and

always has been an illusion. And if that's the

case, what else isn't real?

place. I had spent almost twenty years massaging the idea that this was my life—mothering the ship of my family. I was at the helm, and I had control of the direction. But now that the thing that I of course hoped would happen for all of my children—a healthy and college-bound senior year—had arrived, I was overcome with melancholy and a powerful sense of finality and loss.

There is something about senior year that forces us to recognize the truth: Even though we may have spent twenty years perfecting the idea that we are steering the life of another, it is and always has been an illusion. And if that's the case, what else isn't real?

During my last summer of oblivion there was a barely noticeable, nameless undercurrent of panic, denial, and fear swirling around me. Every mother I knew who had an incoming high school senior could feel it, too. Like the smoke of cigarettes vanquished with other vices of youth, it was formless and wouldn't be contained in a jar to be placed on a back shelf. It would demand attention. Yet nobody talked about it, which made me feel as if my feelings of isolation and doom were my unique problem.

I remember confiding in a girlfriend (whose oldest was only an incoming high school freshman, like she knew anything about the depth of pain heading her way) that I was overwhelmed with sadness thinking about Page leaving for college.

"Oh, don't worry about Page! She'll be just fine," she said.

As if I was worried about Page. She had her whole life ahead of her. I was worried about me. I felt as if the raspberry Jell-O that had held our family of five together was going to dissolve when she plunked her pack on the dormitory bed, leaving only a wet memory of the experience that had been "us." My children's forward movement was going to carry me into empty-nester status with the momentum of a rushing river. All I could hope for was a small spot on the sidelines where I could camp out and reminisce about the years when I was important, too.

What I now know is that your child's senior year is a gift you can enjoy. Really! Sometimes that gift will feel like an unwanted series with a mean personal trainer, but you know the rewards are waiting for you. Or you can just stay Worried Mom, waiting for your daily texts from your college junior, scanning her Pinterest and Facebook posts, and worrying that your twenty-one-year-old was up too late this week. You think I'm kidding? This can be your next stage of mothering. Scary! I believe if you don't address your relationship with your man-child or woman-child during senior year, you are going to find yourself in a big hole that will require a Herculean effort to climb out of. And after the years of this style of mothering have layered a coat of fat and blah on you, you might not find your way out.

August 2012

I haven't seen Billie since we met for a birthday drink on a rainy evening last November. It is a hot summer day when I run into her at Emporio Rulli, where JoAnne and I are looking for an iced coffee after our bike ride. Billie joins us at an outside table and within minutes tells us that her youngest, who transferred from a private high school in San Francisco to the local public high school during winter break of his sophomore year, had to take "three very elementary freshman courses and two PE classes to get up to speed with the curriculum." She puts finger quotes and an eye-roll on the word "curriculum." It was a "ridiculous waste of his time," as the city school was much more academically challenging. She thinks that her son would have done much better in the private school if only he had stuck it out, made new friends, "but what can you [meaning *we*, the collective of mothers] do?"

She told me this same story in November. Ten months have passed, ten months of life, experiences, revelations, and yet she is telling this same story. And it hurts her in every possible way. At least this time she doesn't break into tears. I don't know if I want to hug her or slap her. She asks about my kids, JoAnne's kids. Our husbands might as well be dead. Anyone listening to this conversation would know that we are. Life is buzzing around us, but here we are, old hens clucking about the kids. This is about as life-affirming as picking your own casket—you know, so the kids don't have to worry about it. 'Cause God forbid our children should have to function without us moms taking each and every breath in the service of their lives.

Am I picking on Billie? Don't I have compassion for my friend? As I suck down the last of my iced coffee, waiting for JoAnne's child-activity check-in to end, I'm trying to be kind

"How are *you*?" is what I ask my mom friends now. Believe me, the kids aren't asking each other, "How's your mom?" And that's as it should be.

and to find a generous thought for Billie's mom anxiety. But it's like having compassion for a ghost who has been haunting you for the past twenty years. I see me in Billie, the middle me, the lost me, the me whom I had to say goodbye to if I had any hope of getting back to who I knew I was, who I wanted to become.

Eight years have passed since my first Goodbye Year, and as I look back on who I was then, read my journal entries, glance at photos, all I feel is gratitude for where I am right now.

For years, the first thing friends asked me when we got together was "How are the kids?" They were the common ground of our friendships. During my time as mother of teens, I would reply, "Constantly giving me opportunities for growth!" Yes, we would laugh and exchange stories of our teens' mischief and malaise, bartering our experiences to pick up the better-feeling thoughts that we were not alone. Friendships with fellow moms were the mirror that we could hold up and see ourselves in. That in itself made them valuable. Yet now, some of those friendships have fallen away because those same people couldn't keep up with the woman I was forced to become.

"How are *you*?" is what I ask my mom friends now. Believe me, the kids aren't asking each other, "How's your mom?" And that's as it should be.

But where was I to start reclaiming the lost me? Food. Cooking it, eating it, talking about it, and writing about it has been my life's central focus. Food brought me back to a core of me that hadn't seen the light of day in quite a while.

I've loved to cook since I was tall enough to reach the burners, and I've worked in restaurants since before I was the legal age to do so. We didn't have much in the way of The Law in my hometown, and when my neighbor Mitzie saw how at ease I was with a flame and knives, I got my first job: flipping burgers at her family-owned drive-in. I was twelve. It would be a few years before I'd get to work in the "front" of the house.

My restaurant experience gradually improved as I reached the height (or low, if you count the bawdy uniform) of cocktail waitressing at the Steak and Ale in between semesters at college. Food and restaurants were my touchstone as I leaped from Pittsburgh to Sedona to San Francisco. I met Jeff at his family's restaurant in San Francisco's sunny Marina district when I was interviewing for a job. I got that job and more. Within five years, we were married and opening our own restaurant, Mescolanza, in San Francisco's foggy Richmond district. A dozen years and three kids later, we decided to sell because the demands of a restaurant couldn't exist in the life we wanted for our young family. But by the time I was asked to teach Italian-cooking classes the summer before Page's senior year, I was ready to come out of culinary retirement.

"A cooking class? Who'd come?" I asked my slim friend. "I don't think anyone is eating anymore."

"No, people love cooking classes," she said between sips of Diet Coke, "and you could make some money."

Money, hmm.

"Write up a few ideas. I'll tell the director you'll be in. She's working on the fall brochure now."

I sat at my desk the next day and imagined fun-filled cooking classes targeted to my sophisticated clientele. *Spuntini* and *dolce*, little bites with a sweet ending—they'd love that. Small plates were all the rage. We'd start with *pollo con salvia*, petite chunks of pure white breast of free-range happy hen dusted with flour and roasted with a flock of fried sage. *Radicchio balsamico*, bright-purple cuts of vegetable sautéed with pungent olive oil, splashed with burgundy oak-aged balsamic vinegar, and wrapped in paper-thin leaves of baby-pink prosciutto, finished off with an emerald confetti of Italian parsley.

The next day, before I really had time to think any of this over, I printed out my ideas and headed to the community enrichment office. In my town we take our recreation seriously. Community enrichment is the second-biggest industry, second only to the K–8 school.

Even at a certain age, Priscilla, the director, still looked great in a tennis skirt.

"*Spuntini*, that's a fun word," she smiled, revealing perfectly brilliant white teeth. "Small bites. Everybody loves small plates. This is great."

She liked the idea of cooking something from the cupboard, too. "Really fits in with our busy lives," she said. But her enthusiasm came to a halt when she got to the gnocchi class.

"Hmm, carbs," she tsked. "It's just so, you know, starchy," she whispered sotto voce. "I don't think this one will be very popular—no one's really eating carbs anymore."

I thought about the *panzanella* (bread salad) I had enjoyed for lunch and the *risotto quattro formaggi* (creamy arborio rice with four cheeses) I was planning to make for dinner that night. "Well," I offered, "maybe by November someone will be looking for a potato."

"Sure," she humored me. "We can give it a try."

She had a brochure to finish and a spin class to get to, so we shook on it. I walked out into the bright June sunshine knowing that she thought my Italian spud festival had about as much chance of success as, I don't know, the Red Sox winning the World Series.

With that leap, I started spinning a little story. A story about a woman who, at midlife, launched a cooking-class business that led to a cooking show, fame, money, and happiness. (There was some carpe diem–implied eternal youth thrown in there, too.)

The five of us were going to Italy in July to visit relatives and eat (and drink) our way through Tuscany. I was busy with all the things mothers get busy with when their family is going on vacation. As with a satisfying but light beach read, I didn't give my upcoming classes another thought. Anyway, September was so far in the future, it was hard to imagine.

But September did arrive, and with it reality. I saw the teasing announcement of my cooking classes in an email and decided I'd better pick up a brochure to see what in the hell I'd agreed to do. In my little town, we have to pick up our mail at the post office. Like Mayberry, but with foreign cars and better weather, my village has the small-town dynamic of "everybody knows everybody"—ergo, "everybody knows everybody's business."

The post office is the prime locale where the women of the town check in and catch up. (I did not say gossip.)

My mailbox was jam-packed that day. No surprise. The roll of mail—including a tube that contained Martha's and Oprah's magazines wrapped around *Sports Illustrated*—came out of the box like a birth. In the ensuing paper chaos, my copy of the color brochure slid to the floor. As I bent down to pick it up, Glenda surprised me with an enthusiastic hello. Everything Glenda says is enthusiastic. I think she got her big personality from growing up in Texas and winning beauty pageants starting when she was a toddler.

"I see you're teaching some cooking classes," she said, fanning herself with her copy. "They look *great!*"

All of a sudden it did seem a little warm in there, so I fanned myself with my copy, too.

"Thanks!" I said, trying to muster enough enthusiasm to match her *great.*

The post office was bustling that morning, and before Glenda had a chance to say another optimistic word, Tanya and Melanie were at our side. Hellos and how-are-yous all around.

"Toni, I saw your cooking classes in the fall brochure. I can't wait to take one." This from tiny, freckled Melanie, who loves all things French and Italian, maybe because she is of Irish heritage and, as she once told me, all the meals she knows how to cook are boiled.

"I was just saying the same thing," Glenda piped in.

"What cooking classes?" inquired Tanya as she tossed a long strand of wavy chestnut hair off her face. Tanya could be in a Benetton ad. She is all the beautiful genes of women from India, China, and Africa poured into one tall, supple body.

Melanie, in the know, filled her in. At this point, I was just a smiling spectator. Tanya was delighted to hear about the classes and said she planned to sign up, too.

This was nice. My girlfriends were so supportive. All four of us had a child the same age and had worked together for years. This felt great, just *great*.

After more hellos and goodbyes as busy moms came and went (they should put a bar in the post office), I headed home. In the solitude of my Trooper, I finally picked up my copy of the burnt-orange-and-umber brochure and opened it to the front page. There they were—my cooking classes. Sweet. The ladies of the recreation office were so kind as to place my classes in this very important spot. I proceeded to read the author/chef bio I had sent in with my class descriptions the previous June:

> *Toni Piccinini is the original owner of Mescolanza, a San Francisco Italian trattoria, selected as one of the* San Francisco Chronicle's *"Top 100 Restaurants" and chosen by Michael Bauer, Food Editor, as one of the Top Ten Italian Eateries.*

That part was true. But apparently, in the interest of drumming up a little excitement for the classes, someone had added: *For those who don't know Toni, she is an energy-filled, fun, and vivacious culinary expert.*

Culinary expert! No, I'm not! *Oh, good Lord, what if someone signs up with a big soupspoon up her rear end and asks me culinary-expert questions? And if somebody—some stranger—does sign up, what is she going to expect? Julia Child?*

Or, worse, what if *nobody* signs up?

That worry passed as people—moms—did enroll. And what I got from the experience was nothing like the fantasy I had been fabricating. It was so much better. We shared the months of senior-year milestones together, and the classes and camaraderie kept me afloat. My first six students were friends, five of whom lived in my neighborhood. Which gave me an equal mix of ease (they were my friends) and unease (these "students" were my friends). How was I going to become this other personality—this knowledgeable cooking-class teacher—with women who knew me as, well, me? The teacher had a lot to learn.

The night before my first class, I was sorta-kinda ready. I had stopped by my friend Tabitha's house (mansion) to familiarize myself with the layout of her fabulous kitchen. Tabitha, like many of the mommies of my town, opens her home to end-of-the-year class parties, book talks, and countless fundraisers, and had graciously offered her kitchen as the venue when she found out about my classes. The kitchen in my house (cottage) is one of my favorite places to cook, but if anyone other than Glenda, Tanya, and Melanie enrolled, the phrase "hands-on cooking class" would take on a new meaning. So I had gratefully accepted Tabitha's offer.

My next task, with Page's assistance, was to get the recipe cards done.

"How can you wait until the last minute to do this?" Page asked as she helped me cut the cards and punch the holes for the brad. (I did manage to get to the craft store during the week, and wow—who knew there was so much variety in the world of brads? I selected bronze sunflower September-themed ones for this class.)

"I don't know, honey," I said as I admired my prettily fastened cards, "I don't mean to; it just seems that something comes up every day that's more important."

"You need to learn how to manage your time better."

Well, maybe I would if all I had to take care of was myself, I thought but refrained from saying out loud. Instead I went back to thinking about my fantasy life: Food Network star with paid assistants who would happily punch the holes in my recipe cards and make me a cup of tea.

The opportunity to teach those cooking classes launched the evolution of me. They reminded me that I was more than just a volunteer mom, dedicated to the service of my children. It didn't happen in one day, or even one year, for that matter, though Page's senior year surely forced the issue. The classes also allowed me to see my fellow moms as women.

Those combined experiences have given me the grace of wisdom that I want to share. So here's a handbook of what to expect when you're expecting your first—or last—birdie to leave the nest. Twelve months, twelve little DIY projects, with seasonal recipes to help you reclaim the You of you and send your baby on his or her way. Think self-help cookbook! I'll hold your hand through the college application process, the rejections, the acceptances, and that final goodbye when you leave your child at the threshold of the dormitory and your new life apart begins. But before the school year starts, you have the last summer. Make something sweet.

♡ THE RECIPE

....

Torta della Stagione (Seasonal Fruit Torte)

This torte is great as a dessert, a morning pastry, or even a late-afternoon snack. Like the last summer, it's all good.

WHAT YOU NEED

1 8-ounce box cream cheese

½ cup butter

1 cup flour

½ cup sugar

Best-of-the-season fruit (apricots, plums, peaches, pears, or apples)

Fresh lemon juice

Liquor of your choice

INSTRUCTIONS

This short crust is so simple, *semplice.*

Mix room-temperature cheese and butter together till they fluff a bit, then sprinkle with the sugar and flour. Instant dough!

Press the dough flat with the heel of your hand, and place it on a piece of parchment. If you press it thinly, the *torta* will be crispy. If you leave it a little thicker, it will be soft. Whatever you like. That's the point. It's summer—be flexible.

Now slice the seasonal fruit of your choice and let the slices rest in a little sauce of sugar, fresh lemon juice, and a liquor of your choice. I like amaretto with peaches.

Arrange the slices of fruit on the dough. Drizzle with the sugary-liquory sauce. Crimp up the edges to hold in any juice that might bubble up.

Bake at 400°F until it smells right. Or you can look at it. Okay, let's say twenty-five minutes.

Cool on a rack. Slide parchment to cutting board and cut into squares.

1 · The First of the Lasts

SEPTEMBER

RECIPE: *Coniglio alla Polenta*

"Aren't you just going crazy?" Donna asked in a hissed whisper. Her French-manicured nails dug into my arm for emphasis as she reached across the aisle. It was high school back-to-school night, and we were in the same class. This annual evening takes place at all the schools in our area. Our students bring home their daily class schedule, and we, the parents, experience their day in the form of abbreviated ten-minute class periods. It's like speed school. We meet the teacher, hear a little about the class, and move on to the next classroom when the bell rings. It gives us a sense of how our children spend their days—that is, if they are going to class.

From the front of the classroom, the teacher informed us about what assignments would carry the most weight in AP U.S. History, but Donna and I, like slacker students in the very last row, were more interested in our own historical drama.

"About what?" I whispered back, even though I could have guessed.

"The college apps!" she replied, raising her perfectly shaped eyebrows to convey the gravity of the situation. "Ben isn't working on his essays. I don't know what I'm going to do!"

Before I had a chance to offer her some solace from my platform of seasoned mom with older kids, the bell rang and it was time for me to go to Poetry. Donna was headed to AP French.

"See you at the Lark Creek Inn after seventh period," she said as we scurried off to our high school seniors' next class.

"Okay, see you there!"

Donna and I, along with a group of fellow volunteer fundraising moms, had been meeting for drinks after this annual September event every year since our kids were in grammar school. I didn't share Donna's acute angst about the college apps; Ben was her eldest, but my senior, Banks, was my third go-round. I had earned my been-there-done-that perspective, which took a little edge off the emotions of my last back-to-school night.

But something else gave me a jolt at the event. Even though I didn't have jitters surrounding what to expect from senior year, this year's get-together at the Lark Creek Inn would be another last time for me. When our kids graduated in June, I wouldn't see much of the women with whom I had spent most of the last two decades. We, comrades in amassing fundraising coin, party planning, managing sports equipment, and acting as keepers of the schedules, were about to disband. By the following September, the connections that held us together would be history and, like our seniors, we moms would scatter.

I thought about that in poetry class.

You know how it goes: Your child starts school and makes a friend. They want some after-hours action—a playdate. You introduce yourself to the other mom, and a connection is formed. And pretty soon you, too, have a new friend, new friends.

I remember the first time I was referred to as "Page's mom." I liked it. It was as if I had a fresh, larger identity outside of singular me. Like I was taking a part in a play, playing the character of Page's mom, followed by the encore roles of Ross's mom and Banks's mom.

I realized at that last back-to-school night that my run was coming to an end, that not only would I be saying goodbye to all the roles of Mommy as I knew them, but I would also be saying goodbye to the whole cast of characters who had come to define my life.

Most of us had met when our kids started kindergarten. In my picture-perfect little town, Ross, just a few miles north of the Golden Gate Bridge, the new cedar-shingled mansions blend in with the old cedar-shingled cottages built a century ago by San Francisco families looking for some sun. More than one movie star has made a home here. Many of the women are stay-at-home moms, though ladies in elastic-waist jeans hauling kids around in their minivans they are not. In my town the mommies wear tight J Brand jeans and drop their kids off at school in their Mercedes on their way to sweaty dates with their personal trainers or to the day spa and an anticellulite seaweed wrap. The public K–8 school is the centerpiece of the town, and to keep up with (translation: be better than) the private schools, it holds celebrity author–studded book fairs, tours of secret gardens, theme (Viva Ross Vegas!) parties, and auctions that would impress many venture capitalists. Though some kids head off to the various private high schools in the area, most eighth-grade graduates continue on to the public high school, a.k.a. the zip code high school. The fundraising volunteer moms go with them, a continued connection that keeps the brakes on our collective arrested development.

I realized at that last back-to-school night I would also be saying goodbye to the whole cast of characters who had come to define my life. When our kids graduated in June, I wouldn't see much of the women with whom I had spent most of the last two decades. We, comrades in amassing fundraising coin, were about to disband. By the following September, the connections that held us together would be history and, like our seniors, we moms would scatter.

In 1992, Jeff and I landed in one of the teeny cottages, an entry-level fixer-upper that cost more than all the real estate in my childhood town of western Pennsylvania. Having grown up in the urban fog of San Francisco, Jeff craved the idea of a grassy yard and a sunny, hot summer. Having grown up in the most rural of hick towns, I craved anyplace with sidewalks. San Francisco was working for me. We had started looking at houses just as a form of entertainment, because, come on, we had an acceptable house in S.F.'s Richmond district, our busy Italian restaurant a few blocks away, and a life. But I was pregnant again and full of those easygoing hormones, so before I knew it the baby was born and I was living in the dreamy suburbs of Marin County in a house with three kids—ages four, one, and infant—and the original, 1922 electrical wiring powering the 1987-model baby monitor.

Thus, I suddenly found myself connected to the rich and sometimes famous. Though I always felt welcomed and included, I also felt like I was from another tribe. My restaurant afforded me a flexible schedule, so I could play with my kids and the rich girls, but unlike most of my fellow mom pals, I needed to contribute to the family finances. It was from this distance that I would observe the differences between our worlds, and how, surprisingly, those differences could be erased by the shared challenges of raising children in our time and place.

At the Lark Creek Inn, the drinks had been ordered and we, the mothers of high school seniors, were getting down to business, talking about what was on our minds—The Future. Nobody was in the Now, or in the Know, for that matter. Senior year is the academic version of purgatory, something to endure and pay penance throughout, until the pearly gates of next year's college entrance swing open. And this group of moms was in the thick of it.

Donna shared her constant worry about Ben's lack of enthusiasm for his college-essay writing. After all, it was her responsibility—both to worry and to ensure that he got into the right college. Kate offered a suggestion.

"Just write it for him," she said as she pushed the mint around in her frosty mojito.

"What! I can't do that!" Donna exclaimed from high ground.

At the Lark Creek Inn, the drinks had been ordered and we, the mothers of high school seniors, were getting down to business, talking about what was on our minds—The Future. Nobody was in the Now, or in the Know, for that matter. Senior year is the academic version of purgatory, something to endure and pay penance throughout, until the pearly gates of next year's college entrance swing open.

"Kidding!" Kate said as she crossed her toned legs. "But wouldn't it be easier?"

Kate had a point there. She was a terrific Pilates instructor/interior designer/real estate agent and mother of four. Two were already college graduates.

"I can't remember if it was Taylor or Hunter, but there was so much fighting over all the applications that I hired an essay coach," Kate continued. "It was the best thing I ever did."

"So the coach helped?" Donna wanted to know.

"Sure! He took over my bitching duties!"

Everyone laughed, and the conversations moved on to macrobiotic diets, hypoallergenic dogs, and the dresses worn by the women of *Mad Men*.

Laura was sitting beside me, quiet. She reminded me of me five years ago, when the winds of my first Goodbye Year started blowing in with the start of Page's senior year. Like Donna, she was going through her first "last time," too. And it would be her only one, because her daughter, Bethany, was an only child.

I'd known Bethany since she and Banks were partners on their first-grade diorama. She reminded me of Page. Organized and independent. I knew that unlike Donna, who was going to become a full-time secretary and college-placement counselor for her son, Laura wasn't anxious about the details of the college applications (Bethany would have that covered), but I sensed she was getting hit with the reality that next year Bethany would be gone. She didn't want to talk about it, though. She perked up only when the conversation came around to the winter auction. She was chairing it this last year. Busy, busy.

We all deal with the prospect of change—always inevitable, often unwanted—in different ways. There's the "I'm so busy" approach or the worry-fight-worry approach. I'm personally fond of the denial approach, which is why I plowed ahead with teaching my cooking classes during my first Goodbye Year. I busied myself with this fantasy of my new life (cooking-class diva) even though I hadn't really closed out the old one.

I carried with me a belief that the best years of mothering were past, though I wasn't saying that out loud. Gone were the days of "can't wait to tell Mommy about what happened today." I had plenty to learn about mothering teenagers, not least of which was that it wasn't going to be fun. I like fun, and these kids were turning into a big drag. The energy I put into all the usual

We all deal with the prospect of change—always inevitable, often unwanted—in different ways.

stuff I'd been doing for them their whole lives—binders purchased, laundry done, questions like "How was your day?"—was met with a shrug. Our mother-teen relationships had become typically out of balance. I gave, they took. And it felt like crap. All that was left for me to do as their mother was to nag them. I liked the other way of mothering them. Loving them. Fixing things for them.

But reality does demand attention. In between crafting recipes and teaching my gal pals how to turn on their Viking trophy stoves, I saw in clear focus that every seasonal moment that we shared as a family would be The Last Time. Next fall Page would be gone and the ephemeral thing that was our family of five would vanish. Next fall she'd be off at some fabulous faraway university, having erudite conversations and drinking espresso in tucked-away cafés, and I'd be home doing laundry for her dad and two brothers, cleaning the jack-o'-lantern gunk from the kitchen counter, and getting older.

Getting *old*. I'd have a daughter in college.

Was I jealous of her life, the one not yet lived? Was I remorseful of where I was on the timeline of mine? I held the belief that young people can do and be whatever they want. Try new things on, play around, discard, and change directions. They have all the time in the world. Well, that was my approach. I managed to graduate with a BS in biology. But there was so much more of the academic life that I could have taken with me if I hadn't majored in partying. When my friends talk about Professor This or Professor That, I'm astounded that they can remember the names of those minor folks in the backdrop of college life. I wish I had been a better student. I know now that I missed so much. I knew my daughter wasn't going to fritter away her college years on frivolous things like sororities and parties and political causes. Not like her mother.

That's for sure—she is not like me. She's better than me.

I could see the future. She would head off to college with a strident purpose. She would discover a field of study that would be the foundation of her intellectual life. She would have an intellectual life, and she would stay the course. Again, not like her mother. After my college graduation, I bounced around from one thing to the next—a half-assed attempt at grad school; clinical microbiology bench work; cocktail waitressing; another half-assed attempt, this time at a second undergraduate degree, in journalism; upscale restaurant hostessing; being a travel agent; a second try at research microbiology; restaurant ownership—until finally I landed on the job I was made for: mother. God, I loved being a mom. It was the only thing that stuck.

Whew! What a difference eight years makes! Now Page has graduated from college, and yet I feel younger than I did when she started. You can, too.

It's all in how you choose to handle your child's senior year, come that September. Like Donna, you can spin like a top with worry and claim responsibility for each essay and application,

> Spend a little time playing "he's away at college," because next year at this time he's going to have to go to the bookstore and find the books required for his classes. He's going to have to remember to buy paper for the printer.

or, like Laura, you can make yourself so busy that you won't even notice that your life is about to make a huge shift. But those tactics are like putting a little Band-Aid on the big mommy boo-boo. The first thing you need to do is take a deep breath, settle down, and congratulate yourself for the job you have done nurturing and supporting your child. Mom, you've cared for him, you've loved him even before he was born, and now it's time to just let it be. He's going to land in the right place. And let's face it, you've got your own stuff to deal with.

The second thing you need to do is spend a little time playing "he's away at college," because next year at this time he's going to have to go to the bookstore and find the books required for his classes. He's going to have to remember to buy paper for the printer. Keep that in mind as you inevitably (if you are anything like me) drop everything to dash to the store for that one-inch binder he needs (but forgot to tell you about days ago) for Spanish class this morning!

♡ The Recipe

....

Coniglio alla Polenta (Slow-Cooked Rabbit in
a Rich Olive-Infused Tomato Sauce over Creamy Polenta)

As with the serving after the preparation of *coniglio alla polenta*,
by the time senior September rolls around, you've already done
the work. (Yes, *coniglio* is the Italian word for rabbit, but it's my
experience that chicken works almost as well. And chicken is an
easy substitution for those of you who are too chicken to eat rabbit.) Just as you've lovingly nurtured your child, with this dish
you've carefully selected the best ingredients and brought out
their unique flavor. Now all you have to do is put it on the back
burner under a low flame and it will all come together beau-
tifully, just the way it is meant to—the sauce and your child's
future.

What You Need

1 skinned rabbit, cut into 8 pieces,
or 4 chicken thighs and a full breast,
cut into 4 pieces (skinned but bone-in)

2 sprigs oregano, finely chopped

4 leafy stems sage, finely chopped

¾ cup white wine

3 cups tomato sauce

1 quart broth

½ cup dry-cured black Italian olives

INSTRUCTIONS

The best pan for this dish is a deep, 14-inch sauté pan. I don't use nonstick very often, because I like the food to stick and then to splash it with wine or broth to loosen the browned sticky bits. Cover the bottom of the pan with a nice coat of olive oil and sprinkle the chopped herbs over the surface. Salt and pepper the sizzle.

Once the herbs are dancing, which will happen only if you keep the flame up, place the rabbit/chicken pieces pretty-side down. Don't put a lid on it, and keep the flame up. It's going to make a bit of a mess spattering on the surface of your stove, maybe a little on the floor. If you're tripping about the heat, the sizzle, and the spattering, ask yourself, *Why am I worried about that?* This question will come in handy this senior year with the challenges you'll face and the recipes in this book. Once you're done with the prep part, you can just wipe it up. Okay?

Wait to meddle (I know that's hard, Mom) until the rabbit/ chicken moves when you shake the pan. This signifies that it's time to turn the pieces over. Do that and let the nonpretty sides of the cuts brown a bit. Keep the flame up! More mess is coming. Splash with the wine.

Shake the pan, and with a flat wooden spoon, loosen any pieces that have gotten stuck on the sides or bottom. Add the tomato sauce. (I usually have some tomato sauce canned or in the freezer, but not always. For my money, the best prepared tomato sauce is Pomi.)

Add 3 cups warm water, the quart of broth, and the olives. The olives are important. You'll recognize them by their lack of brine. There's no vinegar. They are dark black and wrinkled like old leather.

Once the very soupy sauce starts bubbling, put it on the back burner, turn the flame to low, and you're done. Let this dish slowly reduce for at least 3 hours. Don't cover it. Start the polenta in the time frame needed to serve it for your dinner hour. Follow the directions on the polenta bag. Right before serving, I like to add a plop of butter and a big soupspoon of grated parmigiana to the cooked polenta. Spoon the polenta and the tender rabbit/chicken pieces and sauce in two oven-warmed bowls. Serve family-style.

 September

The start of a new school year means new friends and some-times saying goodbye to old ones. The September of your Good-bye Year might also mean saying the first goodbyes to some of the roles that you have taken on as mom. With the last back-to-school night dawns the realization of just how much of your social time is spent with fellow moms, whom you met as you settled into your new roles as purveyor of food, school supplies, and clothes, and conveyer of bodies to class, baseball practice, and dance recital. If your child liked another child, you met the mother, and a friendship was formed. That's nice. They're nice. Your friendships are still valid, but ask yourself two questions: Will you spend time with this group after graduation? And what kind of folks might you be spending time with if this had never happened, *this* being your motherhood?

✓ To Do: *Join a New Group*

It can be as easy as taking a class. Are you interested in pho-tography? Not the family-photos-on-the-annual-vacation kind;

I'm talking about black-and-white shots of raindrops pearled on a paned window. Maybe you really know how to apply eye shadow. That's a skill and could be your passion. Take a cosmetics class or volunteer your talents to the makeup department of your community theater and meet like-minded folks. The members of your new tribe may be much older or much younger than you. They may be single, childless, pierced, or Republican, but they will share your passion for the written word, coastal conservation, or a rubber of bridge. Your new group will stimulate a spark in the You of you that has been buried under the weight of years of motherhood. Don't worry. The flame is still there; it just needs some air.

2 · Memories and Melancholy

OCTOBER
RECIPE: *Risotto con la Zucca*

What is it that laces the warm golden light of October with a sense of foreboding? Even without the benefit of a degree in earth science, we can tell that the angles of light have changed and either the sun is turning her back to us or we to her. All around us the colors speak of harvest and a time to tuck in. To tuck in with our memories. October points to the past, and the October of your child's senior year will hit you like the proverbial ton of bricks. And that's okay, because you need to sit with your feelings. The ton of bricks will stop you in your busy tracks. Or maybe you'll plan to pick up those bricks and build a little wall around yourself for protection. If you do that, granted, nothing can get in, but nothing can come out, either.

I remember an October day. I was procrastinating doing my taxes. I always procrastinate that task, which is why I was still not finished a week before the October 15 extension deadline. I talked my slacker self into the idea that a muffin and a *caffe latte* would be just the thing I needed. I did recognize I needed to get out of the house, though I didn't venture too far. My local café's tables were occupied with threesomes and foursomes of

October points to the past, and the October of your child's senior year will hit you like the proverbial ton of bricks. And that's okay, because you need to sit with your feelings. The ton of bricks will stop you in your busy tracks. Or maybe you'll plan to pick up those bricks and build a little wall around yourself for protection. If you do that, granted, nothing can get in, but nothing can come out, either.

young volunteer moms planning the first of many school functions. I couldn't help but eavesdrop. Ideas for the parent cocktail party, the family-day booth, and the class art project for the winter auction were the topics of the day. Those familiar pieces of conversations drifted by my table and stirred the soup of my memories. Was it really twelve years earlier that I had sat here a little anxiously, meeting other kindergarten mothers who would become my committee comrades and friends?

Alongside the planning moms were a few babies cooing in their buckets; at a nearby table, a little girl of three or so was coloring a pumpkin-patch picture. Her mother kept tossing her words of encouragement on her stellar color selection and praise for her precise inside-the-lines technique. Every few minutes the mother would look up from her earnest conversation to confirm that her precious little girl was still there. This mother had nothing to worry about; her daughter wasn't going anywhere. Not for years and years.

Foam and crumbs were all that was left of my latte and cranberry muffin as I thought of Page, my sweet little girl, who was probably at that moment toiling over an advanced calculus problem, not thinking of pumpkin patches or of me. She had begun her senior year with the weight of the world on her shoulders. ACT, SAT, AP, and GPA were her obsessions now. These pressured kids were so far from the days of cupcake dolls and Power Rangers. School had been in session for only a few weeks, but already Page's workload was intense, leaving little room for anything but school, hasty dinner, and hours of homework. It seemed to me her schedule didn't offer many opportunities for joy, and that filled me with regret.

The start of a new school year has always made me happy. When I was a schoolgirl in rural Pennsylvania, it meant new shoes and new stories. The chemical scent of the purple ink from the old mimeograph that cranked out a passage from Jack London's *Call of the Wild* will always smell of adventure to me. The start of the school year held possibilities of far-off places and people, different from the steady stock of honest folk whom I called family and neighbor. And as a mother, after a long, hot summer with three sticky, sometimes cranky small children, I knew the start of school meant some quiet time for me and with it, the memory of the feeling of a new start. Fall is my favorite season, and even though it points to harvest, it has always felt to

Fall is my favorite season, and even though it points to harvest, it has always felt to me like a beginning. This October didn't feel anything like that. All I saw were endings.

me like a beginning. This October didn't feel anything like that. All I saw were endings.

The years of my young life were defined by what grade I was in. I realize now when I give name to a period of time, something to land on as a point of reference, my identity is often anchored by what grades my children were entering then. As Page started her senior year of high school, Banks and Ross began seventh and eighth grades. They'd attended the same school since kindergarten. For these two, school was just the thing they had to do between baseball at recess and lunchtime. College, or any future destination, was only an abstract to them—and to me, too. Page's last year in high school felt ominous, sober, and it put me in such a reflective state that I often found myself staring into space, remembering scenes from my life as though they were being played on a screen. Snippets of conversation, fallen leaves swirling at my feet, or the scent of a roasting bird transported me to another time and place. And I found myself there often, there in the past.

We used to have a morning paper route. My brother, Scotty, was lured into the delivery business by the promise of easy points to exchange for a fishing reel. For me, it was a cream cable-knit fisherman sweater. For Mom, it was status. Herald of the news of the world, she was the "first to know" in our sleepy Pennsylvania coal town. The trouble was, we—not one of us an early riser—weren't very good at it.

Mrs. Gressley was usually the first one to call.

"Debby, where's my paper?" would echo through the heavy beige receiver of our kitchen telephone, which sat near our cups of coffee loaded with cornflakes. (Try that with milk and sugar before you scoff. Spranglin calabro is the name of this hick-awesome dish.)

"The kids aren't there yet?" our mother would respond, with just the right touch of surprise. We all knew that the bundle of newspapers waiting for us on the post office steps was gathering a fine layer of road grit stirred up by the lumbering coal trucks making their way home after the last of the hoot-owl shifts from the Nolo tipple. It would be a while before Mrs. Gressley could read her *Johnstown Tribune Democrat*.

"You know, Debby, that's why they call it a morning paper, so you can read it in the morning. I like to have it with my coffee, and now the coffee's all gone."

"I'll drive the kids over right now with *another* one," my mom would lie, as she had done before and as she would do again and again. While she'd listen to Mrs. Gressley harangue her about punctuality, she'd raise her eyebrows at us, signaling that we'd better knock back the spranglin calabro. Breakfast was over.

That paper route. By the time I left for college, Mom owed the *Johnstown Democrat* almost $600, a small fortune, and she was indentured to the paper route like a double-or-nothing gambler.

The only hope to pay off the debt was to deliver more papers! My dad, out of the loop, questioned why she still did it—it cost more in gas to drive the old Lincoln around town than she could possibly make. Her replies varied from the altruistic "No one else would do it" to the absurd "It gets me up and out early in the morning"—this coming from a manic-depressive who often stayed up the whole night and finally entered deep sleep on the arm of the wingback chair only when the *thud* of newspapers, unheard two football fields away, hit the post office steps at daybreak.

As anxious as I was to escape my small town and start my new life at college, I felt really bad about leaving her with that paper route. There were some early mornings when the buzzer rang in my dorm room, indicating that there was a telephone call for me at the front desk. (As I write this in 2012 I am reminded how archaic my certainly not-coed dorm life must seem to my children and their peers. There was a pay phone on each floor and a sentry at the front desk, whose primary job was to keep the boys waiting in the lobby and off the floors where our beds were.)

"Time to wake up," Mom would say in her singsong voice at six o'clock in the morning, like it was the most natural thing in the world that she would be making phone calls at that hour. I knew that those were the days when the *Democrat* was delivered before even the town early bird, Mrs. Gressley, had her Maxwell House brewing. I also knew those were the days when my mother had been up the previous night and the inevitable crash would come. The next day's delivery would be very late, or maybe not happen at all. The bundle of papers would wait outside the post office until Eleanora Grumbling, our postmistress, lugged them inside so the folks who came to pick up the mail could pick up their paper and talk about the poor job Debby did, especially now that Toni and Scotty were off to college. I didn't want to think about the life she had made for herself, the life that she had allowed to happen, or, more accurately, the life I had left her with. I didn't want to be anything like her. Our connection to the paper route was a guilty one for me and a stubbornly desperate one for her. It occurs to me now, dozens of years later, that maybe she clung to that paper route because she wanted things to stay the way they were, just like I did.

Until the October of my first Goodbye Year, I'd never considered how my mom must have felt when I prepared to leave for college, and by the fall of 2004, it was thirteen years too late to ask her. When I left for the big city of Pittsburgh, she had three children still at home, so it wasn't like my exit gave her an empty nest. She used to tell me that she loved all her children equally, but "you never forget your firstborn." This always struck me as one of the stupidest things she wanted to impress upon me. *Never forget your firstborn? Like you left one in a cabbage patch that you just never forgot about? I'll probably forget about the other three kids I have, but never you, Toni. What?*

"You'll see when you're a mother. You'll see," she would tell me in letters and phone calls over the years when I couldn't put enough emotional and physical distance between us. She was right, of course. Like a prophecy or a curse, I got it when I realized that the days were numbered for my firstborn and me.

In the meantime, I was coming to some realizations about my cooking, too. My goal when I taught the classes was to teach my ladies how to really cook, how to feel their way, not how to follow a recipe. I didn't know I had such an ardent philosophy about cooking until my second class, when I bumped up against a new student who was particularly insistent on exact measurements.

Tanya and Glenda were just getting in the door. Like I do, they had a flexible relationship with time. In front of me, three new students (translation: strangers) were perched on the counter stools. They were definitely front-of-the-class kind of girls, a contrast with Glenda, Tanya, and even busy Melanie, who liked to hover just off to the side in case I needed something. Before I could give them my introduction and an overview of what culinary fun we were going to have, the new girls whipped out pens and paper.

"Oh, don't worry. You don't have to write anything down. I have recipe cards to give you at the end of class," I said, trying to calm my nervous students. Maybe I was trying to calm my own nerves. This was my first class with strangers.

"I always write stuff down when I take a cooking class, because it's the little things you can miss or forget," said one of the front-row overachievers. Pretty in pink, she looked like she had just come from a board meeting, with her smooth auburn bob and discreet white pearls encircled with sapphires in each ear, like a couple of periods finishing off two complete sentences.

"That's a good point," said a newly formed follower of the class anarchist, as she produced a notepad and matching pen from her Prada bag.

"Could we have the recipe cards now? That way, we could write notes on the cards," asserted the student leader.

"Great idea!" said the suck-up.

"I can help pass them out, and I have a few extra pens," said a people-pleasing Pollyanna from the middle of the pen-and-paper trio.

The situation was getting out of control. I needed to lay down the law. But what was the law? Why did I care if they wanted to write things down? Because I didn't want them detached from the food with their pens and notebooks. I wanted these ladies to smell, feel, see, taste, and hear the sizzle. I wanted them to be fully present. My first class, attended only by my dear sweet friends, was a piece of *torta* compared with this bunch. We hadn't chopped a sprig of parsley yet, and I was already being challenged.

"*No, no, no, no, no,*" I said, with such staccato that it came out sounding like some five-syllable Italian word. "I'm not going to teach you how to make a recipe, I'm going to teach you how to cook. The essence of *dalla dispensa* means that you can take what you have on hand and create a delicious meal. The recipe cards are meant to be a guide or a suggestion for your own culinary creativity," I said, smiling broadly as I tried to ooze my Italian-ness onto my slightly skeptical group.

I continued on, putting into words a cooking philosophy I didn't even realize I was so passionate about: "For example, the recipe for today's little tuna cakes calls for a good bit of grated zucchini, but if you don't like that much, use less, or none at all. The pasta I like to use with dried porcini sauce is fusilli, but if all you have in your cupboard is penne or farfalle, have at it! *È non importa!* Though there are some pasta purists who would insist on only certain cuts for certain sauces, exchanging penne for fusilli won't out you as a pasta rube," I confided to them with a smiling wink.

Nothing. They just stared at me. I picked up a bumpy, light brown fertile egg. "See this egg? It will never come again. It's like a snowflake. This day, this heat, this humidity, all of the combinations of this moment are here only once. The food we make today will be special and unique because we're here making it together. So put your pens away and let's get started on the vinaigrette, which is a perfect example of the flexibility of today's recipes." I invited the class to gather round the counter and began handing out cutting boards and knives. Glenda and Tanya were about ready for some morning wine. Me too.

Reluctantly, Prada Girl put her notebook back in her soft, leaf-green leather bag, but Prudence, the leader of the group, wasn't budging so easily.

"I'm just going to keep my notes at my side," she stipulated.

Fine. We got started.

"Before we start the vinaigrette, we need to hydrate the porcini and create the rich, earthy broth we'll use for the pasta sauce," I said in my best I'm-the-boss teacher voice.

I took a full double handful of mushrooms and placed them in a large stainless-steel bowl. The teakettle was almost at a boil. I passed the bowl around so my students could smell the ancient land of Tuscany in the dried porcini.

Before I had a chance to pour the boiling water over the mushrooms, I was commanded to stop.

"Wait! How many mushrooms did you put in the bowl?" asked Prudence.

"For a pound of pasta, you know, a good handful."

"But everybody's hands are different sizes," she protested.

Was this going to go on all class? What was her problem? What was my problem? I knew I had to do something to end this tug-of-war. I wasn't even sure what was irritating me so much, but her need for precision sure was triggering something. There was an implied control in her need for exact measurements. To her, recipe following was cold and passionless, like some science experiment. That rubbed hard against my newly uncovered food philosophy.

Cooking was a creative act of love, a love of the land that produced the food and a love of the people for whom it was prepared. Love wasn't something you could measure. You just dove in and felt it. It wasn't static. It flowed hot and cold, and you just had to go with the flow. You had to be fearless in love and in cooking. And for both to be successful, you had to be present. How could you smell the porcini if you were busy leveling off a measuring cup? Her heart wasn't in it. She was all capable brainpower. A tension was brewing between us: a battle between heart and mind.

"Let's say we use about a cup and a half of mushrooms," I offered as an olive branch. Prudence wrote that down.

"Is that what's on the recipe card?" asked concerned Prada Girl, who I imagined was regretting her decision to listen to me regarding her notebook stashing.

"Yes," I lied, knowing full well that the recipe card instructed a "big handful." Anyway, we'd already covered that.

The class trudged on, and we made some delicious dishes. The presence of Tanya, Glenda, and Melanie rounded out the sharp edges. When Tabitha showed up (to her own house) smelling like eucalyptus from her Phoenix Lake hike, and it turned out that she knew Prudence—they were on a board together—the familiarity warmed things up even more. But something stayed with me after that class.

As we stood around the counter, eating our *gelato affogato*, I retrieved my recipe cards. The night before (still working on that time-management thing), I'd made ocher-colored cards fastened with a pumpkin brad, placed them in clear plastic party bags tied with a terra-cotta bow, and festooned said bags with fresh Italian parsley affixed with my brand, my stickers. Those stickers. Typical of my forward thinking, I imagined that they would be perfect for my cooking class/prepared foods/literary café fantasy business. Not that I had a retail space, or could afford one, for that matter, but I imagined putting those stickers on big handle bags full of stickered containers of my prepared food that my customers would buy when they stopped in to register for classes and book private parties. Surely no one would ask if I had a business card. Not when I could hand out a four-by-four-inch sticker.

"This is so cute," my new friend said as she appraised her parting gift. "It even looks like you."

My logo shows an egg-shaped female with a fry pan in one hand and a goblet of wine in the other. She's smiling broadly, her hair is in a That Girl flip, and her pointed high heels are angled, like she's happily dancing to the beat of kitchen drums. I didn't really feel like that after that class. It had in fact felt like a struggle. For three hours I had felt like I was on the defensive. I still hadn't figured out what was going on, but I knew that I was hanging on to something, and it was growing like a ball of yeasty dough under a warm, moist towel. My casual, easygoing approach to cooking, the very essence of me in the kitchen, had been questioned, and I felt exposed, pissed off, foolish, and sad.

When I pulled into the drive in the Trooper, loaded with my class supplies and another bag of groceries, that October afternoon, I knew that in a few hours a crowd would be forming in my living room to watch the Yankees take Game Four in the American League Championship Series from the hapless Red Sox and put them out of their misery. With the invitation I had promised something yummy, but the prospect of my New York pals hooting and hollering over their domination of their rivals wasn't appetizing enough to get me in the party spirit. I peeled a flaming orange sugar pie pumpkin. I was prepping to make *risotto con la zucca* for the ball game; I couldn't help but think about my class, or rather Prudence. I chopped the pumpkin's hard, golden flesh with angry cuts from my knife.

Good God! What was I so bugged about? All she had done was sit there and ask a few questions. Sit there all buttoned down and organized and perfectly prepared to give her full attention to my cooking class. I imagined that everything in her life was like that. She was always organized and prepared, which translated to the opposite of me. It wasn't much of a reach to finally put my finger on my reaction.

I was jealous—jealous of the focus, direction, and purpose of her every day. I was always flying by the seat of my pants, but Prudence, I was sure, had the world by the cojones. I would bet that her household ran like a Swiss clock. She knew where everything was filed, and she could put her manicured fingers on copies of birth certificates and emergency cards at a moment's notice. All her children's immunizations were up to date, and she got her taxes done in January. Prudence never ran out of toilet paper.

She was the standard to which I aspired, but always, always fell short of achieving. And her insistence on order and a finite measurement of ingredients reminded me of someone.

She reminded me of my daughter.

When I was expecting Page, I didn't realize until she was born that I was expecting a little me. I experienced the first shock when I looked into her blue eyes with my brown ones that this little bundle was not a mini-me, but something all her own. As I watched her grow into a maturity greater than her years, I was often baffled by her reaction to things.

"Why don't you just do XYZ?" I would say time and time again.

And she would reply, "Because I'm not you."

So there it was. Prudence, Page, and even those competent Yankees weren't me. They had it all going on, and I was muddling through, just getting by. I decided right then and there that it was up to me and me alone to change. If I admired the qualities of order so much, I could make it a priority. Even though, after forty-plus years, it had yet to come naturally, there was nothing stopping me from trying harder. I surely had role models to guide me. The irony of taking lessons from my child wasn't lost on me.

"The Star-Spangled Banner" was playing on the kitchen radio, and Jeff and Richie were in the living room, touting the Yankees' greatness with the pregame commentators. I set out a platter of zucchini *dore* and told the boys to wash their hands before they dug in, as I walked to Page's door.

"Come and have some *dore*, honey, before your brothers devour the whole platter."

"I will. I have so much work to do tonight."

Of course she did—she always had so much work to do.

"But you're going to watch the game with us, aren't you?" I was nearly pleading.

"Maybe" was all she could give me.

A few more friends stopped by, and as the pumpkin risotto got gobbled up, so did the hopes of the Red Sox and their fans. I was starting to feel sorry for them. But they weren't exuding despair. Quite the contrary: The Sox were staying true to form, hanging loose, and acting like there was no big panic. I realized that somewhere during that evening I had changed sides. I was rooting for those underachieving underdogs, just to myself at first, and then to the guffaws of my Yankee-loving pals.

The Yankees had carried their 4–3 lead into the ninth inning, and their closer, the great Mariano Rivera, needed only three outs to send the Yankees to the World Series once again. It was a done deal. But then the improbable start of Boston's turnaround happened, with a stolen base. Page joined the party, lured by all the noise we were making. She watched the game to the end, when in the twelfth inning the magic of a walk-off home run won the game for the Red Sox.

Something changed that night. For the Red Sox, it was a magnificent momentum shift that started an eight-game winning streak that led them to a World Series championship for the first time since 1918. And for me, I realized that being true to my nature didn't have to be a losing proposition. Some people, like my daughter, plan well and stay the course. And some people, like me, get a little sidetracked. But as it turns out, we can all reach our destination, no matter how long it takes us to get there or what straight roads or winding paths we choose to follow.

A few days later, I saw Prudence at the dry cleaner. I wasn't completely surprised to notice that I was happy to bump into her. All the irritation I had felt toward her had disappeared with my realization that it was I who had been irritated that day. And she was positively bubbling.

"I am so lucky. I just got the last spot in your November gnocchi class," Prudence exclaimed.

"Yeah!" I replied, a little flabbergasted that she wanted more of my little-bit-of-this, little-bit-of-that method of cooking. We ran to our cars with our plastic-covered clothes hooked on our fingers as the first rain of the season sprinkled the sidewalk. I felt as if more than the weather had shifted. The October of my first Goodbye Year, and the extraordinary baseball season, were coming to a close. Tucked in with my golden memories of that

This month is one of the hardest for the senior-year mom. We know from years past that once the Halloween skeletons are put to bed, it's a race to the holidays. Time flies, and this year it feels more precious than ever before. The flavors of October are best when simmered long and slow. Root vegetables need time to release their sweetness and offer it up to us. The element of reduction comes from the condensing of time. Like a sauce losing its volume under a low flame, time squeezes the moments of your motherhood until all that is left is something small. Small but intense.

fall and the autumns that had come before was the knowledge that those around us can surprise us, and that, more important, if we allow it, we can pleasantly surprise ourselves.

It was the start of me getting to know Me. It would take a while for us to get close and a lot longer for me to treat myself like someone I was in love with. Those old chestnuts with the message of loving yourself haven't lost wisdom just because they've been around awhile. Look at the Bible.

This month is one of the hardest for the senior-year mom. We know from years past that once the Halloween skeletons are put to bed, it's a race to the holidays. Time flies, and this year it feels more precious than ever before. The flavors of October are best when simmered long and slow. Root vegetables need time to release their sweetness and offer it up to us. The element of reduction comes from the condensing of time. Like a sauce losing its volume under a low flame, time squeezes the moments of your motherhood until all that is left is something small. Small but intense.

My friend Connie and I used to make an annual trip to a pumpkin farm, the history of our outing starting when our kids were toddlers. The tradition ultimately morphed into just the two of us, until that fell away, too. On our last trip we talked about the vegetables, our husbands, and, without fail, the kids.

"I remember when I came home from the hospital with Blake and I felt as if my world had shrunk from so large to so small," Connie reminisced over our cups of mint tea, "but inside that small world it was so big." She moved her hands close together and then opened her palms and extended her fingers wide enough to cradle a pint of berries. "Am I making any sense?"

"I know exactly what you mean," I assured her.

Blake, her only child, was a senior, too. When he was born, she quit her job as an executive buyer at an upscale home store. Without even a glance back over her shoulder, she said goodbye to plush business travel to Europe, festive store openings, the

October of senior year is the beginning of the look
back. The house is on fire, and you can take only
what you can carry. You'll want to keep those things
that have been through the crucible—distilled,
reduced, and made richer in quality—while giving
up the great quantities of dross.

adrenaline rush of deadlines, and an identity crafted for nearly
twenty years, all to become a full-time mother. She poured every
ounce of that energy into Blake.

I don't know what it is like to have one child. I had a little
taste of that singularity when Page was born, obviously, but it
wasn't too long before Ross arrived, and before he was walking,
Banks was on the way. I knew what she meant when she talked
about the small world of mothering feeling huge on the inside,
though I imagined the hugeness was quite different for the two
of us. For me, with three youngsters under the age of five, I
didn't have the luxury of the solitary focus that Connie enjoyed.
I used to envy her orderly day-to-day and, sure, secretly dismiss
her worries and moments of overwhelm; I mean, come on—you
got one kid. But that October day at the country café, I felt our
kinship as senior-year moms.

"I don't know what I'm going to do next year," Connie said, putting into words the dark cloud that had been hanging over the Sonoma hills and our playdate.

What would her life be like if she had kept her satisfying job and juggled the career and mother balls instead of putting all her eggs in the one basket? At least she'd have something to fill the void when Blake set sail in less than ten months. If that had been her choice, would she be sitting here (actually, no, she'd be on some pottery-buying jaunt to Portugal), feeling that her only child was soon to leave the nest and that she had missed his irreplaceable childhood?

I thought about all the days I spent hurrying my brood from point A to point B because I had a restaurant to run and was always trying to multitask the three of them into the flow of my work life. So many days I felt stuck with them in tow, like I could just catch the world on fire if only I didn't have these kids to take care of. I tried to straddle both worlds, and in so doing, I rushed right through both of them. Would it have made any difference if I had devoted myself to mothering them 100 percent? As I approached midlife, would I still be sitting here sipping tea, void of regrets?

You know the answer to that. No. There's just no perfect scenario. The moms I know who went back to work after their six-week maternity leave felt like they were robbed of something precious. The moms who took on the lion's share of classroom volunteering and playdate hosting felt like they were missing out on grown-up life. *Their* grown-up life. Not to mention slim skirts and stockings instead of yoga pants and tennis shoes.

So, is it just all bad? No, it's all good. It's life with her yin and yang. It's life with her challenge to seek balance, which is our enduring work. October of senior year is the beginning of the look back. The house is on fire, and you can take only what you can carry. You'll want to keep those things that have been through the crucible—distilled, reduced, and made richer in quality—while giving up the great quantities of dross.

♡ THE RECIPE
....

Risotto con la Zucca
(Creamy Arborio Rice with Sugar Pie Pumpkin)

The thing about making risotto that surprised my students was the fact that it's not mysterious. Most of my ladies had enjoyed the dish in Italian restaurants but were reluctant to make it at home because they thought it was so complicated. It's not. The thing they had to get over was keeping the heat up and allowing the *riso* to completely absorb the hot broth before the next ladle is added.

"We'll never be able to make this again," Prudence said to the group at my Risotto 101 class.

"Cooking is like motherhood, Prudence. You have to feel your way along, but the product will be uniquely yours," I assured her.

As you try this dish on your own, standing at attention at the stove, gradually adding hot broth to the grains of arborio, take the time to be present. Anyway, you have to, or the risotto will end up being just some mushy cooked rice, and it sure didn't get so famous with that attitude. You won't be sorry that you committed to this process. You'll have a platter of creamy, pumpkin-y goodness to share with your loved ones and

Think of the *soffritto* as the foundation of your
relationship with your finished product. In many
ways, it is the same as your relationship with your
child. Like your child, the fresh herbs grow so fast,
you can almost see the leaves stretching toward the
sun. They are bright and wild, and if you don't keep
an eye on them, they can take over a garden. The
bulbs, on the other hand, develop slowly. Out of
sight, they embody what lies beneath the ground,
but they add the most important depth to the
flavor. Like you, Mom. And like life, the oil and the
heat bring it all together.

something to comfort you, Mom, as the days grow shorter but
glow with the golden colors of remembrance.

One of the key differences between risotto and boiled or
steamed rice is the *soffritto*, the flavor base in most of the dishes I
make. For those of you interested in linguistics, the word *soffritto*

is the past participle of the Italian verb *soffriggere*, which means "to fry lightly." There are three constants: olive oil, herbs, and bulbs (garlic, shallots, leeks). And there is the heat that melds them together.

Think of the *soffritto* as the foundation of your relationship with your finished product. In many ways, it is the same as your relationship with your child. Like your child, the fresh herbs grow so fast, you can almost see the leaves stretching toward the sun. They are bright and wild, and if you don't keep an eye on them, they can take over a garden. The bulbs, on the other hand, develop slowly. Out of sight, they embody what lies beneath the ground, but they add the most important depth to the flavor. Like you, Mom. And like life, the oil and the heat bring it all together.

What You Need

2 cups arborio rice

2 quarts broth

1 sugar pie pumpkin, peeled, seeded, and chopped into about 1-inch cubes

Olive oil

Herbs (I like thyme and sage)

Bulbs (garlic and shallots are my go-to, but leeks are nice, too)

Instructions

In a deep sauté pan, add enough olive oil to cover the bottom. Some recipes call for a little butter, too. Sometimes I use it, sometimes I don't. This may appeal to you as culinary freedom or give you anxiety because you want to know what to do down to the half teaspoon. I saw it go both ways with my ladies.

Set the flame to medium, and sauté the chopped herbs and bulbs with salt and pepper. Right before the garlic starts to brown, pull the pan off the flame and add the pumpkin. This addition will cool the *soffritto* a bit and keep the garlic from browning. Stir that around with a flat wooden spoon.

Put the pan back on the flame, and add just a splash of hot broth before adding the rice. Heat the grains of arborio until you can see the tips change from white to translucent. Stir gently and add a ladle (essentially a cup) of hot broth at a time until it is all absorbed. This process will take at least 20 minutes, and you need to stand there. This is crucial, the waiting. Stand there and think. Allow the rice to become almost bone dry before the next addition of broth. You will see the rice give up a cream that is amazing.

Once the grains are somewhere between soft and al dente, turn off the flame, cover the pan, and let it rest for about 10 minutes. Just before serving, stir in a little butter or cheese.

October

There are times when we look to the past as that time when we were *really* happy, and October is the perfect month to time-travel. Kids were little, you were younger, an iced pumpkin cookie used to make everybody's day . . . Sigh, sigh. The changing leaves and golden light are so nostalgic, if you're not careful, you just might fall into the abyss of melancholy.

You need a project. If you are anything like me, you have a box of kindergarten art here, a cache of homemade Mother's

By the time your child reaches his senior year,
your relationship can't help but be cluttered
with the past. Some of that stuff just has to go!
He's not the same guy he was in fifth grade,
but maybe you're still trying to be the same
mother. This is a path to misery.

Day cards there, and photos every which way. Everywhere you look, there is your younger self with your younger child. You need to consolidate and separate the wheat from the chaff. Trust me. Letting go of the broken, colored pasta necklaces and the collections of cotton-ball art will be the best thing you can do for yourself this October.

I know it's hard. I was in no shape to move forward during my first Goodbye Year. That was the last thing I wanted to do. I wanted to resurrect some junk. I was digging around in closets, pulling out old photos (shitty photos with kids' heads cut in half—"Oh, but look! Remember how she loved that Pocahontas dress?"), looking at them to get sadder, putting them back into the box, and then jamming the box deeper into the closet. I don't think you need a degree in psychology to recognize that spending time in this loop of pain isn't very healthy.

Confession: I didn't get down to this task until we moved during my third Goodbye Year.

If you're struggling (of course you are, you're a mom), try that as a strategy. Pretend you're moving. Moving house can be invigorating. It's one thing to keep the clutter out of sight and quite another to look at it, hold it, and feel the weight of it. By the time your child reaches his senior year, your relationship can't help but be cluttered with the past. Some of that stuff just has to go! He's not the same guy he was in fifth grade, but maybe you're still trying to be the same mother. This is a path to misery. Doing this physical task prepares you for the emotional-clutter clearing so you, too, can graduate this June.

✓ To Do: *Make a Memory Box for Each Child*

Clean out the closets, clear the shelves, and collect the best of the best. You can buy a plastic box or craft one out of Alaskan Sitka spruce. Anything to get you moving forward. Load it up with the most precious artifacts of your child's life, but only one box per kid!

Confession number two: I really believe that is good advice (you know, less is more), but I have more than one box per kid. That American Girl stuff was expensive. And the Power Rangers? You just don't throw away Power Rangers. Do your best and consider this a work in progress. Keep what you can't bear to part with right now. Release the rest to the universe, and I'm telling you, not only will you feel better, but something good will come rushing in to fill the vacuum (maybe that volunteer job will turn into a paying one).

I've found that as each year passes, it gets easier to let stuff go—literally and the other way. Anyway, do you want your kids to have to do this when you croak? "Why did she save all this junk?" they will intone over your dead body. *Poor, pitiful Mom,* they will think. Unless you had a little *Bridges of Madison County* action—in that case, make a box for you, too. That will spice up the funeral.

3 · Gratitude Is a Fickle Friend

NOVEMBER
RECIPE: *Gnocchetti di Patate Dolci*

The act of making gnocchi is a powerful antidepressant. When done with a group of women, this culinary task connects us to the ancient goddesses of kitchens past, who wave their magic wands over us. Ah, serotonin.

The ladies in my November cooking class were feeling it as we riced, rolled, cut, forked, and arranged the heavenly potato-and-spinach pillows on parchment-lined baking sheets. But we hadn't even gotten to the eating part when the spell was broken.

"What colleges does Max have on his list?" Melanie asked in her soft little voice.

It was as if a dam had burst. Everyone started talking at once.

"His counselor has him focusing on only his top fifteen."

"Bethany's writing coach says that she should expand her list."

"Who are you using for an SAT tutor?"

"We started the visits when Sam was a sophomore."

"The college counselor at the school is okay, but we also hired an educational consultant, just to be safe."

For the rest of the class, all the potato-fingered moms could talk about were the college application essays—the essays were one *more* thing that we moms had to make sure were getting done. Deadlines were approaching faster than the last of the autumn leaves were filling up the gutters. In California, the UC application deadline is November 30. It comes up like one of those things that you know intellectually but don't really *know* until it hits you upside the head, akin to the November realization that darkness is the color of each early-morning and evening commute.

The banter continued. The focus was on safety, as in the opposite of peril. Safe. These moms' kids were safe from a danger I didn't know existed, or maybe one that I refused to believe was there.

It started when Page was a sophomore. The Angst. The Worry. The Dread. Page and her smart posse of friends were convinced that getting into a *good* college was going to be a feat that would require constant attention, and its attendant stress was just part of the process. I had a hard time believing that was true. When I was in high school, the horror story told at sleepovers went something like this: "It was only that one time [prom night, usually], and they didn't *really* go all the way, but . . . she's pregnant!"

Page's nightmare tale was a little different: "She had a 4.2 GPA and a 2350 on her college boards, helped a small Central American country gain independence during her summer internship, and . . . she *didn't get in!*"

I wanted Page to relax. She was a terrific student. There were so many colleges; she would have lots of choices. When other families were making early visits to New England to scope out the best schools, we loaded up the Trooper and drove to Tahoe for a little family skiing. When parents were scheduling essay-writing sessions with solid coaches, we were going to a baseball game. Page was already so busy with her AP classes and the extra classes she was taking at the local community college that I thought she would be better served with a little "don't worry, be happy" atmosphere at home.

It wasn't like we had never talked about the college apps, but Page was so organized, I knew she had it covered. In September, I had asked her if she wanted to take an SAT prep class. She had replied that she already had so many classes to worry about that it would be just one more thing to do. Sounded good to me.

But the spirited dialogue at my gnocchi class gave me a jolt. It was something like the November Grim Reaper's admonishing finger pointing straight at me: *You loser, what the hell have you been thinking? You suck as a mom! If her hopes are dashed this spring by a pile of rejections, we know whom to blame. You. You and your la dolce vita, everything's-gonna-work-out horse manure!*

I knew I had to fix this. After hearing what all the good moms were doing, I felt that I should have pushed more, been the right kind of mommy, like my ladies, who acted like adults and took charge of their kids' lives, and not the wrong, easygoing kind I'd always been. I needed a chance for redemption.

For the rest of the class, I was only partly there, worrying that I had really screwed up this time. I couldn't have known then that everything was in place for a reason, and that sometimes we find the answers where we least expect to find them.

That night, over a dinner of slow-roasted pork and polenta, it really felt like winter. The rain tapped on our kitchen windows, the eighty-year-old wavy glass panes steamed up from the heat of the oven. The boys were getting steamed up thinking about what might be waiting for them in the mountains. Snow, glorious snow.

"Let's go skiing this weekend," Jeff suggested.

"Yeah!" the boys exclaimed in unison. They knew that most weekend trips to our family double-wide in South Lake Tahoe included an early Friday exit, and I could see the wheels turning in their heads. Maybe they wouldn't have to study those spelling words after all.

"I can't," sighed Page. "I have to work on my college essays."

My prayers had been answered.

"I'll stay home, too, and help you," I exclaimed.

"You can't help me," Page shot me down. "I have to write them myself."

I wasn't going to be deterred.

"Well, of course you'll write them, but we could have a writers' workshop weekend. I'll finish my story, you start your essays, and then we can, you know, workshop them. It will be so much fun."

"Yuck," said Ross.

"And then we can take a break from all our hard work and get a pedicure and go to the Bistro for duck confit." I was on a roll, painting the best mother-daughter weekend ever.

"Yuck," said Banks.

"Shut up, Banks," said Ross. "Why are you always copying me?"

"You shut up, Ross," countered Banks. "You didn't invent 'yuck.'"

"Boys!" Jeff bellowed.

"It might be nice to have a girls' weekend," Page said.

Thank you, boys.

We cleared the plates, and I took the stuffed Sebastopol apples out of the oven. The comforting scent of cinnamon, raisins, and caramelized sugar smoothed out everybody's sharp edges. While we watched an episode of *Star Trek*, we ate the apples with a scoop of vanilla-bean ice cream, which melted down the sides of the stretched red skins and cooled the first hot bites of roasted fruit, making a creamy sauce in our bowls. It was one of those moments that would make a permanent home in my memories of what it was to be a family.

My second gnocchi class, which followed our mother-daughter college application weekend, was easier than the first one because my anxiety had lessened for the time being. Page was doing a fine job with the essays and applications, which (temporarily) silenced the voices of my *you aren't doing a good job as a mom* demons.

We made the same piles of potato and filled the same trays with "pillows from heaven." The ladies enjoyed the tactile activity and were relatively relaxed, even though it was the Monday before Thanksgiving.

"Are you cooking?" was a repeated question, and "Hell, no!" was a popular refrain. But the group was divided between the turkey chefs, who wouldn't have it any other way, and those who were delighted to order everything from the gourmet grocer or go to a family member's house.

After we made trays of the traditional white-potato gnocchi, I showed them how to make sweet-potato drop gnocchi.

"This dish could be your new sweet-potato food-group requirement for the Thanksgiving feast," I suggested to my class.

"Oh my God!" Tabitha exclaimed as she tasted her first bite. "I am definitely going to make this. Bob will love this. It tastes exactly like the gnocchi we had in Umbria last summer, and God knows he'll need something to make him happy. Thanksgiving is insane since his only sister married my first ex-husband."

"How in the world did Bob's sister meet your ex?" asked one of my new students, also one of Tabitha's board-member gal pals.

"Rehab," said Tabitha between bites of gnocchi.

That seemed normal enough. Conversation bounced around the table, centering mostly on everyone's plans for Thanksgiving dinner, the family members who were coming, and the ones who were not. Two of the ladies had college freshmen who were making the cross-country trip home to California from their snowy campuses.

At the mention of college, a flurry of questions similar to the ones that had so unnerved me in the first gnocchi class a few weeks earlier came on like a sudden storm: who was applying where, and who was working with whom, mixed with testimonies about the moms' struggles to get their seniors to finish the applications on time.

"Where is Page applying?" Tabitha asked me as we cleared the empty platters of gnocchi and prepared for dessert, oven-roasted pears with a mound of *cannoli crema*—fresh, sweet ricotta with flecks of mini dark chocolate chips. I ticked off her short list.

"Those are great schools. You seem pretty calm compared with the moms of seniors I know," Tabitha said as she dug into the caramelized surface of the pear. "What's your secret?"

I knew that I was smiling like the *Mona Lisa*, but I couldn't help myself. The memory of our college-apps weekend did that to me.

Jeff and the boys did leave for Tahoe the Friday after my first gnocchi class. I was so excited to have Page to myself. I was going to get some stuff done, too. Writing, reading, writing again. I could smell the productivity in the sharp November air. I wondered if we'd even be able to sleep with all the energy we would be making from the creation of writing. Of course, we would need to eat, you know, just to stay alive.

"Where do you want to have dinner?" I asked Page when she got in the Trooper after school that day. I was already feeling bubbly, having jettisoned two boys and one husband off for the weekend and looking forward to a houseful of female juju.

"I don't care," she replied, dropping her twenty-pound back-pack on the floor with a *thud*. This was her default response. *Do you want to walk to San Anselmo for a cappuccino? What movie should we rent? Do you want to go shopping? What would you like me to cook for dinner?* It seemed that the answer was "I don't care" more often than not. I didn't know if she really didn't "care," or if the effort to become engaged wasn't worth it. I spent so much of my energy caring about all kinds of things, I was always trying to infect her with my exuberance.

"How about the Bistro? We could walk over after we stop at the movie store."

"I thought we were going to do work."

"Sure we are, but we have to have dinner. And I was thinking that since it's Friday, maybe we should just relax with a chick flick tonight so we can get an early start first thing tomorrow." That sounded like a plan to me.

"You don't do anything first thing in the morning," she reminded me. "Anyway, I have some math homework to finish before I start the essays."

How was it that I had a daughter who was able to shrug off a chance to goof off like the bad idea it was? I dropped her off at home, drove to the market for a few staples, and picked up a movie for later. As evening approached with the early dark-ness that November brings, I popped some organic white corn the old-school way (on the burner), drizzled the fluffy pile with melted butter enhanced with black truffle oil, and topped it off with pink sea salt. I opened a bottle of Sonoma syrah—a perfect pairing with popcorn—and invited Page to join me.

"Look at these essay questions," Page said. She slid them across the kitchen counter. "I don't know why they don't just use the common application. This popcorn's good," she added. At least I had done something to take her mind off her heavy workload.

I looked over the questions. They seemed like fun writing prompts to me, though I had nothing riding on the quality of the answers. Most of the colleges included their version of "Why our school?" among the obligatory "If you could have dinner with anyone . . ." and "What is your unique feature?" essay questions.

"Can't we watch the movie now?" I asked Page, like she was the parent.

"Okay," she said, giving in to my inner child.

The next morning, we sat at our separate desks and wrote. Page came into my office from time to time to show me what she had been working on. The longer essays were versions of assignments she had completed for her senior exposition class. They had a thesis statement. There were no spelling errors. They were grammatically correct. They were earnest. And I imagined that they were similar to the other thousands of essays college admissions committees were receiving and reading (plodding through with double espressos) across the country.

"Honey, I think that you should go out on a limb. The admission counselors who read these are probably women my age, and believe me, they would love to read something funny. Everybody likes a little humor. Let me try one."

Page was applying to a college with a pretty name in Tennessee. I suggested: *I don't really know much about your university or your state, but I just saw* Cold Mountain, *and W.O.W., if the boys in Tennessee look anything like Jude Law, count me in!*

She was thinking about a school in Illinois: *If I were honored to represent your university to the world at large, I would be proud to call the great state of Indiana my home. Oh, just kidding—I know it's in Iowa!*

"Why are you so crazy?"

"It's not crazy. It's funny. You know the not knowing what state it is is patently absurd from someone as clearly intelligent as you are, evidenced by your test scores. And you know, Jude Law, Tennessee, he's British . . . It's funny," I assured her.

"This isn't *Legally Blonde!*" she reprimanded me.

"Look how well that did," I reminded her, "and anyway, what's with you and these snow schools?"

"Oh God! Everybody makes such a big deal about the weather back East. I don't see what the drama is all about. I've been to Tahoe. You just wear a coat!"

"Now that's funny." She was cracking me up. "Maybe an essay about your California-girl snow experience will warm a heart in Chicago this December."

She did just that. She wrote a funny weather essay and included my Pennsylvania-mommy reaction to her Tahoe line. We did get to the Bistro on Saturday night, and by the time the boys returned from Tahoe Sunday afternoon, the first round of applications were ready for the post office. The boys were starving and dug into the rigatoni with braised chicken thighs and portobello mushroom sauce I had made earlier in the day. We ate our bowls of pasta in the living room, in front of the Sunday-night football game. Ross and Banks told Page their tales of daring, and she teased them about their acute boyness. The rain had let up, so Jeff and I took a little after-dinner walk with Indy, the air as fresh and creamy as sweet lemon chiffon.

"How was the weekend?" he asked. "Page seems relaxed."

"It was wonderful."

And it was, because of much more than the satisfaction of getting the job done. Page and I had connected as opposites, like best friends. It was a joy for me to see her change gears and open up to the endless possibilities she had in front of her, and to the good times she could have experiencing this moment. The weekend also gave me a glimpse of the future, of what a woman-to-woman relationship with my daughter might look like. The emotion I felt was simple, *semplice*. I was grateful. For months I had been looking only over my shoulder, at all I would miss, but now I had a new vision, a first taste, of what might lie ahead for Page and me. It was delicious and left me craving more.

I love stories of the slightly depressed heroine who has an epiphany, a lightbulb moment when she breaks out of the sludge she has created and moves forward, never looking back. I think that's just in the movies. It sure as hell wasn't my experience. My momentary emotional expansion was fleeting. The ten-years-down-the-road future might end up being just dandy, but for now I was still stuck in what was.

The following weekend, the round-two essay questions weren't so funny.

"Let me see those prompts," I commanded Page. She was working on/suffering through the short-form essays for the last three colleges on her list. She had joined me for a cup of tea to take a small break from the grind.

"Why do they ask such stupid questions?" she lamented, as

> The inherent weakness that runs to the marrow in a mother's love is that we will not allow anything to stand in the way of the needs of our offspring. Even if our own sense of self may be at odds with what is necessary to keep them comfortable.

she read queries from "What is your Achilles heel?" to "What have you outgrown and what have you found to replace it?"

I thought about the first prompt (after I flashed on an image of a totally ripped Brad Pitt playing the role of that Greek hero) and that spot of extreme vulnerability we moms share. The inherent weakness that runs to the marrow in a mother's love is that we will not allow anything to stand in the way of the needs of our offspring. Even if our own sense of self may be at odds with what is necessary to keep them comfortable. Yes, I have three Achilles' heels. Everything in my world can go along swimmingly until the smallest of arrows—a perceived injustice, a rejection, an argument—flies in and pierces any one of my three soft spots.

What had outgrown its usefulness? Was it that obvious? I had!

Plus all the things that I thought were important to mothering: placing the children first, being available constantly, and thinking of the impact my actions—what I said, what I chose to wear—would have on their world. Not to mention every mother's most important job: worrying.

Meanwhile, the kids, for the most part, aren't even aware of how grateful they should be. Sure, you might get a "thanks, Mom" for dropping everything you're doing to drop off the forgotten history book, permission slip, or baseball bag, but after a lifetime of being the center of another's attention, they just expect it. And from regular experiences of expectations fulfilled, it's only a short hop to a position of entitlement. Nobody plans to have a kid oozing entitlement, but it's a natural side effect of giving too much. Another, even more insidious side effect of this pattern is that our life disappears and we become a supporting character in our child's life.

We never stop being mothers, but we do allow our personhood to take a back seat. The November of your Goodbye Year, get back behind the wheel of your life. Nobody is going to do this for you. Feel grateful for and celebrate the fact that you can still drive.

You, whether you realize it or not, have outgrown your need to do everything for your child. More important, your child had better outgrow his dependence on you this year. (Remember the "he's away at college" game?) But be forewarned: Nobody wants you to change. Why would they? You're so manageable this way, doing things for them, blending in, being a supporting character.

My friends who were willing to talk about this prickly dynamic just accepted it as motherhood. Yeah, they complained, but they didn't think there was anything that could be done. What choice

Nobody plans to have a kid oozing entitlement,
but it's a natural side effect of giving too much.
Another, even more insidious side effect of this
pattern is that our life disappears and we become
a supporting character in our child's life.

did we have? Be selfish? Let the kids fail? Heavens, no! Well, I took that all in. No doubt it was cathartic to hear I wasn't the only one who had lost myself along the way, but it wasn't encouraging to hear my fellow moms resign themselves to this shadow role.

When you're walking in a snowstorm, it's hard to calibrate the distance you are covering. The white is everywhere and the pace is labored. You have a good day, hours when you feel authentic and connected to yourself. Then you see your reflection in your child's eyes, and you are once again reduced to a single dimension—mother. The November of my first Goodbye Year was another stop on the road of my long and slow transition from mother back to woman. What started the process? Awareness. Challenging my long-held beliefs about mothering and "womaning" with this one question: *Why do I think that?* ("That" being the thoughts of a lifetime congealed into a belief system.)

Over a lifetime of building a family and playing these roles,

When you're walking in a snowstorm, it's hard
to calibrate the distance you are covering.
The white is everywhere and the pace is
labored. You have a good day, hours when you
feel authentic and connected to yourself.
Then you see your reflection in your child's
eyes, and you are once again reduced to a single
dimension—mother.

I'd been thinking all along. Lots of it was incredibly mundane:
Is there an extra roll of toilet paper in the guest bathroom? And
some of it was scary: *Do I still love him?* There is much solace in
pretending. Even if the comfort zone is unhealthy, it's familiar.
But by allowing myself to finally acknowledge that it wasn't so
great, I became able to question how I was living my life, first to
myself, and then out loud.

Your partner and kids are completely invested in Mom being
Mom. They won't be all, "Oh, wonderful. Thanks for pointing
out what's wrong with everything." They won't like it. Too bad
for them. You don't need their permission to get reacquainted
with who you are. If October gave you an introduction to the

If October gave you an introduction to the You
of you, consider November the beginning of
a new love affair. Being a mature woman, you
take it slow. No drama—it's not puppy love.
Treat yourself like you've just met You, and you
are very interested in this mysterious woman.

You of you, consider November the beginning of a new love
affair. Being a mature woman, you take it slow. No drama—it's
not puppy love. Treat yourself like you've just met You, and you
are very interested in this mysterious woman. For me, a clear
marker of time, our last year as a family, was the spark I needed
to set fire to all that I had outgrown. It's a good thing I started
then, because by the time my third little birdie was ready—or
not—to leave the nest, I felt comfortable enough to chart my
own new flight plan.

That's not to say it's easy to change course altogether, especially not when Thanksgiving—an entirely tradition-bound
holiday—happens this month. That particular November, I
repeatedly asked myself how I could be in such a crappy mood
during a time when joy was supposed to fill the countryside. I
thought I was the only ungrateful, bitchy mom in town. Turns

out, we were all suffering. Because the sameness we were clinging to for dear life was also something that had outlived its usefulness, and we knew it. We knew it in the place of our deepest
wisdom, though the knowledge had yet to make its way to our
consciousness. All around us the Past was relentless, insinuating
itself into the here and now, while the focus of the senior year
was the Future.

Without a game plan, this paradox can drive you crazy.

"I had an epiphany today," Kate told me when we ran into each
other at the grocery store. It was the Tuesday before Thanksgiving, and already the parking lot was packed. My free-range
heritage turkey hen was in my cart, along with all the fixins for
the fixins.

"I'm going to make a pork roast for Thanksgiving," Kate
announced. "It just hit me. I've been stuffing that fucking Wil-
lie Bird for the past twenty years, and I'm done. All that work,
and no one has ever shown any gratitude for my effort. It took
me until today to realize that nobody in my family even fucking
likes turkey. The boys [she had four of them, not counting her
husband, Bob] don't even like mashed potatoes!"

"Hey, it's like you could have had a V8!" It was a treat to run
into Kate with her pants on fire, dropping f-bombs like an Irish
sailor.

"No fucking kidding. I was in such a funk this morning thinking about the next two days, but once I picked out that piece of
pork, it was like the clouds had lifted. I feel great!"

"You look great, too." Kate always looked great. She was a
Pilates instructor, after all, but I could see something else ema-
nating from her countenance. Authenticity.

"Happy Thanksgiving," we said in unison as we made our way to the checkout lines. I had plenty of time to think about Kate's newfound verve as I inched forward in the slow-moving line. Glancing at all the magazines with golden-brown turkeys on their covers, I wondered how many other women across the country were having some of the same feelings that Kate had discovered this Thanksgiving week. My guess: a lot.

I remembered the dominant theme of the conversations that had swirled among the ladies in my cooking class the previous week. Everyone was talking about what they were doing for Thanksgiving, and it struck me that the "have-tos" and the "shoulds" were the anchors of many of the plans. And, no surprise, most of the hostesses were not looking forward to the fete—nor, frankly, to some of the guests. There was Connie's uncle Merle, who made sexist and racist cracks that no one could stand; Glenda's sister-in-law, who would badger everyone with statistics of misery related to her latest cause; Tabitha's brother, who would be three days out of the slammer for failure to pay child support—not because he didn't have the funds but because he loathed his ex-wife and wanted his kids to know their mother was a bitch who would send their dear dad to jail. In every case, my friends, my fellow moms, felt that it was their responsibility to smooth out the impossibly rough edges of family.

Year after year, we try to make everything okay for everybody, especially for our kids. You know it's impossible. Ha! That's why nobody else is trying to do it. This year, give yourself a break. You don't have to leave your irritating relatives out in the cold, but you can ditch the ownership of them. Allow them to be who they are, and treat them to a taste of who *you* are.

Unlike Kate, you don't have to abandon the sacred bird of our

Year after year, we try to make everything okay for everybody, especially for our kids. You know it's impossible. Ha! That's why nobody else is trying to do it. This year, give yourself a break. You don't have to leave your irritating relatives out in the cold, but you can ditch the ownership of them. Allow them to be who they are, and treat them to a taste of who *you* are.

Pilgrim ancestors, unless you don't like turkey either, in which case, go for the goat! What you can do is make a small shift in your routine. It may seem silly, or just symbolic of the change you'd like to see in your world, but these minor steps are revitalizing. And isn't Thanksgiving a celebration of the bridging of two cultures? Pilgrims and Indians, in-laws and outlaws, mothers and women, little you and divine *You!*

♡ The Recipe

· ·

Gnocchetti di Patate Dolci
(Sweet-Potato Dumplings with Gorgonzola and Crispy Sage)

Go out on a limb and shake things up this Thanksgiving. Instead of your tired old sweet-potato whatever-the-hell-you-make every year, make this sexy Italian version. *Gnocchetti di patate dolci* will fill the kitchen with the seductive aroma of fried sage. Turn on some Italian music and tie on a playful apron.

"What's gotten into Mom?" you might overhear your less-than-grateful family members ask.

What You Need

Olive oil

Fresh sage

Coarse sea salt

2 big fat eggs

1 15-ounce can organic sweet-potato puree

Salt

Nutmeg

White pepper

Flour

Gorgonzola

Instructions

Heat some nice olive oil in a sauté pan.

Drop in many leaves of fresh sage. Remove the leaves just when they start to turn color. They will get as crisp and delicious as a potato chip. Place on a plate with or without a paper towel, but save the now-sage-infused oil and set aside.

Sprinkle the leaves while they are still hot (the salt will stick better this way) with sea salt.

Whip the eggs. Add the sweet-potato puree and a pinch each of salt, nutmeg, and white pepper.

Add enough flour to make a batter that resembles a thick cake batter.

Drop by teaspoonfuls into a big pot of boiling, salted water. When the gnocchi float to the top, remove with a slotted spoon, tap out the excess water, and place the seasonally appropriate, colored dumplings on a warmed platter. When all are cooked, drizzle with the reserved sage oil. Crumble gorgonzola over the little orange pillows. Top with crispy, salty sage. Serve with turkey, pork, or goat.

November

Most likely you will have some family get-togethers this month, and most likely you will be doing the work. Your senior will be too busy to help you because she will be working on her college essays. Sometimes it's hard to feel grateful when you have bills to pay, a sinkload of dishes to do, and clothes spinning in both the washer and the dryer. Instead of answering the "What are you grateful for?" question with the usual things outside yourself, try this: *What qualities/talents do I possess as an individual that I am grateful for?* And when you're giving thanks, don't forget that the enjoyment of the holiday is yours for the taking, too.

Today, I am grateful that I have an answer for one of Page's college-essay prompts: "What have you outgrown and what have you found to replace it?" I have outgrown my need to be everything for my kids, my need for them to think that I am the perfect mom, my need to make every holiday celebration everything for everybody. So, what replaces all that? Me, just me, another imperfect woman, who happens to have three kids for whom I am—yes!—so grateful.

✓ To Do: *Start a Gratitude Journal*

The serendipity of writing down even the most insignificant things that you are grateful for is astounding. Your journal can be something as humble as a leftover spiral notebook the kids have discarded or a leather-bound beauty. You might enjoy some artful creativity and decorate the cover with fabric, pretty paper, and ribbons. In any case, give yourself the gift of gratitude.

Start close in. It's easier than you might imagine: *I am so glad that Jeff left those two tablespoons of milk in the gallon so I could smooth out the acid of my coffee this morning. I am so grateful that my dog threw up and pooped on the hardwood instead of the carpet.* See what I mean? There's always something that makes us feel grateful. The power and magic of writing it down is an experience not to be missed.

I'll give up a little secret: The more you find to write about, the more you find to write about. When all that gratitude attitude is circling around you like a tornado, the layers of worry and "shoulds" will start peeling away, and what will emerge, like the butterfly from the cocoon, is the You of you.

4 · Ghosts in the Photos, Devil in the Details

....

DECEMBER
RECIPE: *Italian-Hawaiian Ham*

My friend Mary Ann has a special dress that she has worn every Christmas Eve for as long as I've known her. I think she planned her two pregnancies around fitting back into that dress. And every year she lines up the Christmas photos—twelve of them!—with her in the dress and the kids getting older and older (thankfully, wearing different clothes). It's as if she is stopping time with that constant—her in the dress. But she's not.

There's no holding December back. It's like a determined freight train barreling down the track, sounding a warning whistle that can't be ignored. Yes, December will have its way with us, and before the month is through, there will be no hiding from the fact that another year has passed. And for you and your college-bound senior, the finality of the year's end will resonate more strongly than ever before. If you're paying attention, all the familiar celebrations of faith, family, and food will take on added significance.

December will have its way with us, and before the month is through, there will be no hiding from the fact that another year has passed. And for you and your senior, the finality of the year's end will resonate more strongly than ever before. If you're paying attention, all the familiar celebrations of faith, family, and food will take on added significance.

The ladies of my December cooking classes were in the thick of it. Their conversations focused on travel arrangements and how to fill the days during the winter break, right alongside a frantic feeling of *there's not enough time!* A paradox. They were coming and going, spinning in place, but no one was standing still.

"Belize," Glenda said for the second time when I asked her what she was doing for the holidays. The first time she had responded to my question, I had thought she was saying, "Please!" (as in, *Puh-leeze don't get me started on the hectic life that is the American holidays*).

Tanya and her clan were headed to the mountains, Melanie to La Jolla. It never occurred to me to leave for Christmas! I thought that being a good mom meant giving my children a secure memory that they could hold on to. A scene they could conjure up when they were toiling away at their college library, wishing that last final were done so they could come home. That's how it was for me.

The Decembers of my childhood were filled with the sweet energy of anticipation. Everything that happened after Thanksgiving was in preparation for Christmas. School activities were packed with card and gift making, play rehearsals, and decorating the classroom with construction-paper chains of red and green. Choir practice at church heated up with the challenges of six-part harmony. Housecleaning took on a competitive fervor. And then there was all the cooking and baking! Nut rolls, poppyseed rolls, fig- and prune-stuffed "horns," birds' nests, and biscotti were made, covered, and stored in the basement larder. Caramels with walnuts were wrapped in little squares of wax paper and set in tins with the precision of masonry. I guess it was stressful, but in those days the fun *was* the stress. We country folk created it just to have something going on.

And how I used to feel sorry for the poor, unfortunate souls who wouldn't have a white Christmas! How could those people in California stand it? Growing up in western Pennsylvania, years before global warming, meant a lack of snow for the entire month of December was never a concern. I came of age with an abundance thereof.

Memory is a funny thing. Every family has its own stories that it trots out to give voice and texture to the clan's identity. Each family's individual humor or pathos sets it apart, even as the stories tell of common ground. Our memories of what actually happened blend with stories that have been told about those events, and through the prism of the mixture the recollection morphs, reforms, and takes its place on an important shelf in the museum of who we are.

Sometimes a trigger brings forth a strong memory that we may have thought was long forgotten. The smell of baked pineapple roasting atop a clove-studded ham does that to me.

And there she is again, my mom, Deborah Mae Kinkead Bassaro, sitting at the kitchen table in her robe, smoking a Winston, the dregs of her Maxwell House in the bottom of her cup, engrossed in a story from the *Reader's Digest* condensed books of the month.

My mom was an only child of divorced parents, which must have made her quite an odd bird in our tiny town of immigrant coal miners. In the late 1930s and early 1940s of her youth, she lived in the biggest house in town with her maternal grandparents. Nana, Mom's mom, was off to the state capital with husband number two, and a nine-year-old girl just didn't fit in with the parties and politics.

Great-Grandfather was the superintendent of the mines, which made him the richest man in town. Hence, Mom lived a Shirley Temple childhood with loving grandparents, a widowed aunt, and occasional visits and frequent gifts from her glamorous mother. As her maiden name suggests, she was not Italian. She met my father's sister, Assunda, at a scrap-metal drive—as Aunt Sue tells it, "And there's Debby Kinkead, throwing her old bicycle onto the heap"—before she met my father, who was away in the South Pacific. He had lied about his age and presented a sketchy birth certificate so he could wear the uniform of his new country. I imagine the U.S. Army wasn't too picky in 1942. Aunt Carmella told me that Mom fell in love with the idea of his loud, large Italian family before she fell in love with him.

"It was her downfall," Aunt Josefina liked to point out.

Mom had a small arsenal of WASPy dishes that she had watched the help make in her grandmother's kitchen, but the recipes she learned from my father's sisters were the staples and the stars of our family dinners. Mom took to her new family with a grand thirst of belonging. Learning to make the food of her husband's heritage became her mission. And helping her became my assignment. We were on par in terms of our domestic duties by the time I was seven. As the oldest of four, I used to think that being an only child with a grandmother and an aunt doting on me, with no competition for their affection, seemed like the life of a princess. But Mom talked only of the loneliness, and she took every opportunity to remind me how lucky I was to have two brothers and a sister to babysit while she got her hair done.

Every December the sweet, smoky smell of cloves, pineapple, and ham melded with the aromas of the tree's crisp pine, Uncle Frank's cigar, and the impossible combination of ancient and fresh on the powered cheeks of the great-aunts. The layered scents filled the air of our house like a long-awaited guest, and it was Christmas.

I imagine that the Hawaiian ham must have been all the rage to the postwar housewives of my family and town, given its exotic—and expensive—ingredients, its beautiful presentation, and the pure Americanness of this modern cuisine. It also spoke to a paradox in the immigrant kitchens of my aunts and neighbors. Food was as large a part of their identity as their language and religion were. Their connection with the old country could be tasted in the sauces bubbling on their stoves; their link to their history was palpable in the feel of each different kind of pastry dough they made. But they also shared a desire to be a part of this great, adopted country, and I think that making a home for a dish that was on the covers of magazines did that for them. Thus, for every Christmas I can remember, alongside the ravioli and the *baccala* and the biscotti, sat the Italian-Hawaiian Ham. And like a good immigrant woman, I brought it all with me to California.

Every Christmas I make the same dishes that my mother and aunts made year after year. I hold fast to the need that my children "know" who they are and where they come from, and feeding them the food of my childhood is the medium I choose to teach them this information. If love can exist in the crunch of hazelnut biscotti, so can memory. The repetition of Christmas food rituals is my connection to who I am, and the repetition of my children's rituals—"the tree goes here"—is their connection to their short past.

As the Christmas of my first Goodbye Year approached, I planned (as usual) to give my children what they had learned to expect: Cookies packed in tins tucked away in the downstairs fridge, nut and poppy-seed rolls wrapped twice in plastic and foil, and the distinct smell of the decorated ham that had crossed cultures, generations, and the continental United States would be my gift to them and to myself. Like western Pennsylvania's Rolling Rock beer, I would give my family the steady, "same as it ever was" Christmas that I thought they cherished. That I thought *I* cherished.

But that December I was starting to feel a thorny contradiction that felt as out of place with my vision of another holiday season as the first Hawaiian Ham must have looked in Aunt Jo's Italian kitchen. The sameness that can be such a comfort can also feel stifling. I thought of Glenda. Christmas morning she would be on the beach, her warm skin glistening with coconut oil (eating a lo-cal fish taco that some handsome Belizean stranger had made for her), and who knows, maybe next year she'd be on safari. Perhaps that was the way to do it. If you just kept moving, you might not notice that things were changing.

Yeah, and so what if things *were* changing? Of course they were. Certainly, living in the past wasn't the ticket to happiness, nor was it going to stop the momentum of life. All this tradition that had seemed so important to me the year before—and every other year, for that matter—suddenly felt like an overstayed visitor. It wasn't like I could keep everybody home and happy (and eternally young) with a few cookies. So I decided I was moving into the future, and whoever wanted to come along for the ride was welcome. I knew just the vehicle that would take me. I decided I was going to follow through on a magazine-inspired idea of my own. I'd wanted to do this for years, and that December I exercised my housewife's prerogative.

In the past I'd caved when my ideas—a frosty vision of icy blue and silver reminiscent of a Russian *Doctor Zhivago* Christmas, or a red-velvet-and-gold Victorian-inspired nod to Charles Dickens and the poor but happy Cratchit family—had been met with four loud refrains of "No way!" Too bad. This year I was busting out. I was going to have a theme tree.

"Only the ornaments that are red, white, or blue," I instructed Ross when he started to help me decorate the tree.

"But what about the three mice?" Ross asked.

"Nope. They're red and green."

"But we put them on the tree every year," he protested.

"Put 'em back in the box."

"Mommy is having a *theme* tree this year," Jeff said, stating the obvious and offering up his already-established opinion of my creativity with his sarcastic stretching of the word "theme."

"I thought you guys were watching motorcycle crashes on the Man Channel," I tossed back at him.

"It's over," Banks said as he came into the living room. He reached for one of his favorite ornaments—a gold-and-green lanyard elf guy he had made a few years ago.

"Wrong colors, buddy," I said as I took it off his hands.

The rain outside was a presence. There were pings in the gutters and plops in the driveway. These were the sounds of a California December, and mixed with the light neighborhood traffic, they became an orchestra. As the cars drove by, the layer of water on the street yielded and gave way to the power of the steel and rubber. The crescendo and decrescendo of the water parting and returning under the tires reminded me of the ocean. But not the crashing of waves. It reminded me of the portable sound of the ocean found in the giant pink and polished seashells that I used to listen to in the landlocked Pennsylvania of my youth as I dreamed of a life somewhere else.

No doubt here I was, living that dream life of *somewhere else*, the perfect somewhere else of Marin County, California, with a husband and children all safe and sound.

The rain was urgent. Dusk was closing in, but even in the gloom the yellow of the poplar trees outside our windows reflected what little light there was and magnified it, held it, concentrated it. This storm would knock off most of the golden leaves that still clung to their branches. By morning, the space created by their letting go would reveal more of what was in the distance.

The boys—all three of them—finally left me alone to decorate "my" Christmas tree. They were in the garage, trying on moto-cross gear that Jeff had found at the sports consignment shop.

It seemed that as the boys moved solidly into their adolescence, Jeff was keen on joining them. I guess we were all doing a little time traveling that December.

Just as I placed the last bouquet of dried sky blue hydrangea on the boughs of the tree, I heard the front door bang. Page entered the foyer on her way to the kitchen, fighting with her umbrella, her backpack pulling the sleeve of her raincoat over her shoulder. She was home from the night class, calculus, that she was taking at the local community college—her high school college, as I liked to call it.

"Is there any dinner left?" she asked as she dropped her heavy load on a counter stool. She had had to rush out the door to get to class on time. The final was that night.

"Sure, honey. Sit down. How was the final?" I thought I might as well get it out of the way. Either it was a "disaster" or it was "okay." It was never "no problem, I aced it, I'm on top of the world!"

I heated up creamy tuna penne and made her a plate of pasta and sautéed spinach. She sat down at the kitchen counter and sighed, "Thanks." Turned out, the test was "okay. I'm just glad this class is over." She looked tired. She was paying a price for her aspirations, and there wasn't anything I could do about it. The advice I offered—"You don't need to put so much pressure on yourself"—was not accepted. I didn't know what I was talking about, and all my concern did was send our conversation in a testy direction. I had learned to just be supportive and let her spin out with all her work stress. Well, I was trying to learn to do that. It was a work in progress.

"Where are the boys?" she asked after a few bites of my winter comfort food had warmed her.

"In the garage, trying on helmets and padded shirts. And

tinkering with those motorcycles, I imagine. They look like Power Rangers. Daddy, too."

"Guys!" Page said as she rolled her eyes.

"I know!" I said in female communion.

As soon as she finished her dinner, I shepherded her into the living room to feast upon my creation.

"What do you think?" I asked her as I proudly stood aside my red, white, and blue creation. "It's my Take Back America Tree."

"You named the tree?" she said. It was more an accusation than a question. She looked at me like I was crazy, like everything I did was something that she would have to deal with, process, and judge. Another burden pressing down on her little seventeen-year-old shoulders was the fact that she—and she alone—had a mother who gave name to a Christmas tree.

I hadn't set out to name the thing, but when I was at the fabric store, looking for something rich and "magazine-y" to replace the natty old tree skirt, I came upon a flag-patterned cotton that reflected my color scheme. Draped around the base of the tree, it reminded me of the bunting Mary Todd Lincoln used for all those Civil War fundraisers, or maybe of the decoration on the backstop of the All-Star Game. In any case, I liked that Americana-cornball look (you can take the girl out of the country, but you can't take the . . .), and it just took off from there.

The previous November, my candidate for president—the Democrat—lost, and I took it personally. Democrats, particularly California Democrats, were soundly dismissed on the national scene as a wacky, harmless fringe at best, and as unpatriotic, protesting traitors at worst. That December I took a stand (even though the stand was only the red-white-and-blue-covered Christmas-tree stand). I wasn't going to take it anymore. I was the daughter of a World War II vet who had served his country along with five of his brothers. We were all lifelong Democrats and proud of it. For me, that year's Christmas was a season of reclaiming, and putting a name to the spirit felt just great. I'd start off small—reclaiming the country—and then move on to the bigger stuff. My life.

The winter holiday started the next day. The last day of school was a blur of classroom parties, the exchange of secret-Santa gifts, and the early exit of travelers who were out the door right after lunch. I shared a hug and a "happy holidays" with Glenda and Tanya as they herded their kids into their packed SUVs—Tanya's Porsche Cayenne loaded with skis and fur, Glenda's with snorkel and golf gear and presumably the thong bikini she had talked about in cooking class. Thankfully for Melanie, who was picking up her kids at the same time, and who has strong ideas about what is and is not proper for a mother, Glenda wasn't flying it from her antenna as she left town.

The relief of the end of a semester lifted Page's spirits, and when I picked her up after school, she was game to do a little shopping with me. The radio in the Trooper was set to 96.5, the Christmas-music-all-the-time station, and we sang along with Mariah Carey's "All I Want for Christmas" (a guy) and the Wilson sisters' "Hey Santa!" (bring me a guy) as we happily crawled along in the Friday traffic, with no deadlines to fret about. Dan Fogelberg's song "met my old lover at the grocery store . . ." came on. It was the first time Page had heard it, but for me it was a flashback to my college days.

"And the snow turned into rain," he sang as the saxophone cried and faded away into "Auld Lang Syne."

"That's so sad," Page said.

"I know, but I really like it."

"Me too."

The yearning for something past and lost seemed to fill up the car. It was only seconds before the mood shifted, but in that brief quiet space, as time thickened and slowed, I knew that I would always remember that moment. Even though I was overcome with the emotion of the *memory* of emotion, and the knowledge that I would never feel the way I did when I was younger, I was aware that Page was right there with me. It was as if we were sharing the same feelings. How could that be? She was too young to know what it was like to even *have* a past, but maybe on some cellular level she knew that this was a last Christmas. Maybe she already knew there would be lines in her life that would mark time, and she was crossing over one now.

I am a nostalgic person who can get carried away by the scent of drugstore cologne (kissing Ricky DeMarco under the bleachers) or by the smell of nighttime snow (kissing Mokey Long in the church parking lot), but I don't know why that song always stopped me in my tracks. It's not like I had an old lover for whom I still pined. "The snow was falling Christmas Eve" evoked more than a memory of past passions. It was the memory of the possible. And what I pined for was the old me. What I pined for was a complex of "old mes"—the me I had been when I was Page's age and had everything opening up ahead, the me that had reveled in marriage and small children, the me that had made a family and a home for twenty years. And maybe the mes that could have taken a different path. . . .

The bone of the ham shank rocked in the simmer of the stockpot, creating a culinary humidity that filled the house with the scent of smoke, onion, and clove. Before I had consigned the Holiday Hambone (not me, the other one) to the pot, I scavenged for the bits of remaining meat that clung on tightly. The close-to-the-bone morsels are always the sweetest, and I excavated just enough ham to make a carbonara for dinner that night. By the next day I would have more than enough rich stock to make a warming Tuscan bean soup that would serve as the ritual meal to mark the end of Christmas.

It was New Year's Eve Eve, December 30, and the guys were downstairs, watching college bowl games; Page was at the mall, exchanging the blouses I had given her.

"They're so cute!" I had exclaimed when she tried them on Christmas morning.

"Yeah, if I was heading out to my law firm."

God, it used to be so easy. I could delight her with a T-shirt, a nightgown, a pair of socks decorated with hearts for February, shamrocks for March. And I spent so much time on this stuff. The button-up blouses, in shades of very hip petal pink and sky blue (to match her eyes), were rejected in less time than it took me to choose the tissue paper that lined each box. It surely wasn't her fault. I thought I was trying to adapt, but I was helpless against the pull of the past. I was addicted to being Mommy. I wanted that rush again. I wanted to feel the absolute power that came from being the most benevolent queen in the kingdom of my family.

I could tell that Jeff noticed I was struggling. How could he not have, with all the sighing I was doing? He had given me such thoughtful Christmas gifts: German knives, French perfume, and Italian candies. I read into those choices that he was telling me there was a big world out there. But I was in a self-imposed prison of my memories of what was, and I needed to serve my term.

I wrapped up the last of the delicate (red, white, and angel blue) ornaments and put them in their boxes. I like taking down the tree and clearing the decorations. After a few hours of work, the house feels bigger and ready to move into the new year. And that year, I relished the idea of chucking that bastard tree.

In an effort to be more sustainable—still didn't have a compost pile—I had bought a "living tree." How wonderful to start a new family tradition of using the same tree year after year! We'd bring it in each December and marvel at its new growth. At the end of the holiday season, we'd take it back outside, where it would live with its cousins, the redwoods. Maybe over the years we'd buy a bigger pot to hold it. How we would cherish our living tree! It would be like having another dog, but one that didn't poop.

Yeah, that was the plan. It could have worked if that douche bag tree weren't so combative. The first time it bit me on my derriere, I forgave it. Must have needed more water. The second time the prickly needles drew blood, I shot back with an Italian "Are you talking to me?" It crossed the line with the third attack. Full of Christmas cheer, I enjoyed watching that demon tree die of thirst. It would take its place on the curb with all the other dead evergreens waiting for the chipper—only ours had a root ball to add to the mix.

The lure of food brought the football-saturated guys upstairs. Page called, had run into a friend—no doubt exchanging gifts *her* mother had spent hours selecting—and said that she would get something for dinner with her gal pal. Jeff opened a nice montepulciano, the red wine a sharp contrast with the smooth linguine carbonara. The boys took their bowls of pasta back downstairs to the TV, leaving Jeff and me alone in the steamy kitchen.

We fear the unknown just like our ancient ancestors did. They decided to light some candles, huddle around the fire, and while away the darkness with stories and togetherness. We modern moms keep the wolves at bay with activity. And one of our favorite activities is worry.

"Are you making any resolutions?" I asked him.

"Are there some resolutions you want me to make?"

"Very funny, but you know there is always something we can set out to improve about ourselves."

"Well, thank God I have another day to get my list together," he said, giving me his usual sarcasm with a smile on his face.

With December and 2004 ticking away, I thought about what I would like to accomplish in this upcoming new year. Aside from the usual "exercise more, lose ten pounds," I had no idea. I felt stuck, and I didn't have the energy to want anything other than for everybody to stay stuck with me. When the clock struck 2005, it would be the year Page was leaving, and I was afraid of the future.

We fear the unknown just like our ancient ancestors did.

They decided to light some candles, huddle around the fire, and while away the darkness with stories and togetherness. We modern moms keep the wolves at bay with activity. And one of our favorite activities is worry.

We think about possible outcomes, land on one that we don't like, and fret about it. It goes round and round. *What will happen if he doesn't get in? How am I going to pay for this if he does? What will happen if she isn't happy at her dream school next year? What will happen if he can't do the work without me? What will it be like around here next year in this empty house? What dress will I wear (after all the extra December calories have left their mark on me) to the New Year's Eve party? OMG, what are the kids planning to do that night?* Worry, worry, worry. Fear, fear, fear.

There is only one antidote to all our fears and worry, and it is a beautiful balm. Faith. Faith, with its power to reduce fear to the sniveling nothing that it is. Faith is the December vibe. We share the community of faith with our sisters and brothers all over the globe. The specifics may be different in our practices, but the commonality is there. We want to believe that everything will turn out okay, that we're doing the right things, that there is some higher purpose to all this. But faith without trust is a sticky spot. We *say* that we "just want him to be happy" no matter what he chooses to do with his life, but what we *mean* is that we want him to get into Dartmouth, get a good job, and make a life for himself that we can understand. We understood what made for a happy life for him when he was a child. We are hanging on to our idea of what that will mean in his future. Now, we may need to stretch our understanding of what a good life is. The only way to do that, Mom, is to place your trust in your faith. There's an expression I've picked up from a lifetime in (and out of) church. It doesn't matter what religion you practice; the truth of it is uni-

Faith is the December vibe. We share the
community of faith with our sisters and
brothers all over the globe. The specifics
may be different in our practices, but the
commonality is there. We want to believe that
everything will turn out okay, that we're doing
the right things, that there is some higher
purpose to all this. But faith without trust is
a sticky spot.

versal: If you're gonna pray, don't worry. If you're gonna worry,
don't bother praying. And that's what putting your trust in your
faith means.

In my box of Christmas decorations there lives a photo, too. Like
all photos, it snapped a moment in time and held it. We are at a
ski resort. I stand taller than all three of my children. I am wearing slim black ski pants and a hunter-green fur-trimmed jacket.
The belt is cinched. I look happy and sexy. I will never look like
that again. I know you know what I'm talking about. Not too
many years passed before that photo was bumming me out so

much that I left it wrapped in tissue to hibernate in the bottom of the box. I didn't want to be reminded of happier times.

I used to think that photo of me as a young mommy with my three little chicks under my wing made me sad because of my vanity. Now I know it was because as the children grew and grew up, my role as their protector and provider was slipping away. It was wonderful being so needed by the three of them. I knew just what to do to keep them safe and happy. But as the years passed, confusion supplanted the confidence of early mothering. The three little kids in that photo adored me and trusted me completely. The three teenagers they had become . . . hmm, not so much. Hadn't it been just a few years ago that they'd peppered me with questions: *Mommy, why doesn't it snow here? Why can't Indy have puppies? What's the month between March and May?* I'd had all the answers, and they had never doubted me. Even my sketchy weather-related knowledge. But now?

"Oh, Page, you are going to get into any college you want," I'd say with clear confidence when she'd start fretting about her list.

"No, it's not 1975 anymore," she'd reply to remind me that my experiences were obsolete. Or maybe that was just my take on her healthier, more realistic outlook. Senior year gives our kids a taste of the endings of things, but they are not afraid of the future. What colors it for us moms is the knowledge that their future is our past.

Now, eight years later, I look at that photo and feel trust moving in the other direction. That's the gift. They had faith in me in their child world, faith with trust. And now I have faith in them. Real faith with real trust. They know what they are doing. They will make mistakes. And they will learn. The three children in the photo weren't worried about stopping time, or even

> Senior year gives our kids a taste of the endings of things, but they are not afraid of the future. What colors it for us moms is the knowledge that their future is our past.

slowing it down, because they weren't afraid of what might be coming their way. Children are naturally present. The gift of time is theirs for the taking.

This holiday season, be brave and be faithful to yourself. Wear your faith on your sleeve. You don't have to be afraid to be You. Be in the present this holiday season while you remember the love and joy of Christmases past—even if you don't have a Dickens-inspired tree. Over the years I have let go of many of the traditions, but not that ham. The wafting scent of spice and smoke filling up our home is the essence of Christmas Eve to me, and, I hope, to my children, too.

♡ THE RECIPE

• •

Italian-Hawaiian Ham

The ham I bought this year cost $65. Sixty-five dollars! It was about ten pounds (bone-in), and it was $6.50 per pound, but I'll tell you what: It was worth it. And I was happy to support the local pig farmer who raises and cures his hams the old-school way. We ate it for days, and then I made gallons of hammy-clove broth to freeze. Give yourself this gift, too. A naturally cured ham was just like the ones I had as a country kid, and the taste: like going to bed on Christmas Eve and hearing reindeers prancing on your roof.

WHAT YOU NEED

A beautiful ham (I like the shank and I like the bone),
not one that is spiral sliced

Whole cloves

Pineapple slices, canned, juice reserved

Maraschino cherries, some juice reserved

Mustard

Brown sugar

Toothpicks

A baster

INSTRUCTIONS

Preheat the oven to 325°F. With a sharp knife, slice away the "pigskin," or the parts that look like a football, but don't go too crazy cutting away all the fat. The slow-roasting and melting fat is part of the alchemy.

Score the ham by making circular shallow cuts—less than a quarter of an inch—spaced about 2 inches apart, east to west and north to south. You should end up with a checkerboard pattern of approximately 2-by-2-inch, shallowly cut "boxes" decorating your ham.

At each intersection or corner of the "boxes," insert the stem of a whole clove to a depth that shows the clove on the surface. In other words, don't bury the clove. This will take a lot of cloves.

Depending on the size of your ham, you may need a can and a half of pineapple slices. Start at the top and place the slices all over the clove-studded ham, securing with two toothpicks per slice. Place one bright-red cherry in the center of each pineapple slice. Secure those with a toothpick, too.

Place the ham in a baking dish with a size and depth similar to that of a broiler pan. Make a basting sauce by warming the reserved pineapple juice in a saucepan. Stir in the brown sugar, mustard, and a splash of cherry juice to taste. (The approximate amounts are 1 cup pineapple juice, 3 tablespoons mustard, 1/2 cup brown sugar, and 2 tablespoons cherry juice.)

Drizzle/pour the sauce over the ham and bake for about 3 hours. Every 20 minutes or so, baste with the drippings.

To serve, arrange the browned and shrunken pineapple slices and cherries on a platter alongside thinly sliced cuts of the best ham you've ever tasted.

ꙅ December

Holidays celebrate our connection to the past. During the Good-bye Year, those connections can feel like a lifeline one minute and a stranglehold the next. This holiday season, take a break from the past and give the future a rest. Enjoy a little *now*.

✓ To Do: *Give the Gift of "Time"*

And I don't mean a Rolex. I like cashmere sweaters as much as the next girl, but a date with a loved one warms me up from the inside. Buy tickets to a basketball game or a reggae concert, a cooking class (shameless self-promotion) or a lecture, and schedule in time with your senior. He might protest a "date," but if it is for an event that he'll like, such as monster-car wars, you will get the pleasure of his company (and you just might discover your inner NASCAR fan). Give yourself the gift of time, too. Ditch some of the "have tos" and schedule time for activities that are exclusively for you—activities that will build the future you are moving toward.

5 · Diets and Denial

JANUARY
RECIPE: *Pastina*

I stood there in my little white socks as the crisply lab-coated young woman kept inching the hanging weight farther to the right. She had started the measure where I had left off a little more than two years ago, the last time I'd visited Dr. Yee for my "annual" visit.

"How many pounds since the last time I was here?" I asked her on my way to the potty.

"Twelve," she replied matter-of-factly.

Damn! I should have peed first.

Twelve pounds was a bunch, but when I did the math, that translated to less than half a pound per month. That didn't seem like that big a deal, I reasoned. But I wasn't alone in my ob-gyn's restroom as I came to that conclusion. Tinga Uno and Thing Two, my Italian and Anglo advisers, were at the ready to give me their two cents.

Don't worry about it, you look great, and so what if you're a little softer, you deserve it, you're fifty, for Christ's sake, and look how nicely you fill out that bra.

Are you kidding me? Twelve pounds on your petite five-foot-one frame. Get serious! Get on a diet, and get back on that NordicTrack, and while you're at it, clean up the dust that has gathered on your old friend.

You're a woman. Embrace it, enjoy it, this is what a woman looks like.

Oh yeah, this is what a middle-aged frump looks like. Is that who you are now?

Leaving those two behind with the samples of prenatal vitamins and nipple creams, I headed to the exam room. Tall and elegant, Dr. Yee strode in wearing Burberry ballet flats and gave me a warm hug.

"Toni, so nice to see you. How long has it been?" she asked as she flipped the cover on my chart, and then answered her own question. "Two years."

When I was pumping out babies, it seemed like I used to see her every week, but as the years passed, the interval between visits stretched out farther and farther. Dr. Yee is my age, and we collectively had our five children during the same time frame. We caught up on our kids' lives (naturally!), and then she wanted to know how I was doing.

"Oh, a little blue, you know, with this being Page's last year at home, and a little tired, but other than that, fine."

"Are you still working out?" she asked, focusing her attention back to my chart. All my vital medical information, collected minutes ago, was right in front of her. I was right in front of her. Was that another one of those doctor questions—the answer obvious?

"Well, not so much, but I'm still playing tennis," I replied as I tried to put some lilt into my voice. Not that the brand of ladies' doubles I had been playing lately was really much exercise, I thought.

"So, you're tired, a little blue, and I see that you have gained some weight."

"Mm-hmm." I'd seen the commercials. I knew where she was headed. I could have been the poster girl for the "Lady, You Are Depressed—Get Some Pharmaceuticals and Snap the Hell out of It" campaign. The "before" picture of a lumpy, sad hausfrau (me) could dissolve into a perky, trim, happy sexpot (me a hundred years ago) with the aid of a modern-day Mother's Little Helper. Dr. Yee seemed to be connecting the dots, and I could feel a diagnosis coming on.

"Depression is a common occurrence at this time of life," she continued in her doctor voice, "but you don't have to go it alone." Then she switched gears like she was offering me a cocktail. "I could prescribe something for you."

"Oh, I'm not depressed! I just need to exercise more."

"Exercise is great."

"It sure is!"

We left it at that. Looking back, I can see that I was in such a rut I couldn't even imagine what it might feel like to feel better. I was accepting the weight gain, the blues, and the low energy as a condition I deserved because it was of my own making. And I was resisting any help. All the while, I was trying to keep up with the people-pleasing part of me that had lost authenticity. It felt like the tags of all my clothes were made of boar bristles, and tugging at them to ease the irritation was taking most of my limited energy.

The January drizzle came down on me as I darted to the Trooper and drove home over the Golden Gate Bridge. Even the weather was ambivalent. The rain was voluminous enough to be too much for the intermittent windshield wipers to handle, but not enough to provide the lubrication needed to accommodate the pace of the wipers' low-speed setting without my having to endure the screeching sound. My choice was between the two tandems of irritating noise and clear vision, or soothing metronomic swipes and the dangerous interval that came with it when I couldn't see five feet in front of me. I went back and forth.

Finally back in Marin, I headed to the market to pick up a few things. My first soups class was coming up, and I wanted to try a twist on the classic *pallottoline in brodo*, little meatballs in broth. I could imagine my ladies being tempted by the richness of the beef yet relieved that the addition of fresh, local greens would add zest, vitamins, and scant calories to the soup. I was going to teach them how to make an almost custard-like *pastina*, a dish that every kid on Earth loves, and a hearty Tuscan bean–and–winter root soup that I was planning to whip up for the football playoffs. "Guys love a bowl of this in one hand and the remote in the other," I would tell my devoted students, and we would laugh!

I was looking forward to another spate of classes, set to start later that week with the soup lesson. It had been only a few weeks since December's cookie-making class, but those few weeks—the winter holiday—had seemed like a few months. My teaching was the one thing in my life that seemed to be moving in the right direction, and I missed my ladies and our camaraderie.

I thought about a couple of new recipes, and before I knew it I found myself with a cart full of milk, eggs, butter, pasta, cannellini, parmigiana, prosciutto, pancetta, cambozola, and fresh-baked ciabatta.

Thinking of my ladies and the connections that were growing in our classes lifted my spirits. I had started the day in a funk—the doctor visit and the January drizzle sure didn't help—but after focusing my thoughts on what yummy, soupy creation I'd make for dinner, I was feeling a little better, not great, but good was good enough. It was at that moment that I ran into Sydney, or someone who looked like half of the Sydney I knew.

"Toni, hi! How are you?" this thin, lively person asked me.

"Happy New Year," I replied like someone who was just learning the language and had a few key phrases under her belt. Yeah, like I was wearing a belt.

"I hear your cooking classes are a blast! I can't wait to take one once I'm off the jicama diet," said the woman who sounded like Sydney.

Indeed, four Cryovac-sealed packages of julienne cuts of this miracle white vegetable were the only thing in her cart. She turned and reached for another package. I guess the twisting and tippy-toes action I was witnessing was the exercise part of the diet. I couldn't take my eyes off the backside of her chocolate-brown pants. Where her ample rear end had once been were two undersized pockets with outsized flaps, each sporting a considerable button that held the flaps in place. Underneath the decorative pockets appeared to be two beautiful, perfectly formed mounds—small, petite mounds—of muscle.

What happened to your ass? I did not say, but instead offered, "You can still be on a diet and take a class. They're so much fun, and the dishes we prepare are really healthy."

Our eyes met at the junction of my food-as-spiritual-nourishment philosophy and the tsunami of fat-ass cart shame that crashed over me when she glanced at what I was packing.

Her charm bracelet jingled when she looked at her watch and exclaimed that she had to go. Off to her world of sparkle and light.

"Great to see you," the new, improved Sydney said as she trotted off like a young filly. She reared up at the bottled-water aisle, leaving me behind. The emotion that filled me up like a coconut milkshake does not have an English word to accurately express it. This was not the first time I wished I knew German, because I was sure they must have a word for the crappy reaction I was experiencing. This was the opposite of schadenfreude, the pleasure one feels at one's enemies' failures. This was a mix of jealousy and awe one feels for a friend's accomplishment of something that we think we desire but are not willing to do the work to succeed at, and that we are pissed off to see her do, especially because we know she is so freaking pleased with herself.

Sydney was exuding serotonin. She was a happy pheromone–making machine. But that brand of happiness was a cheap knockoff of the real deal. Nobody is happy when she's starving.

I tried to talk myself into feeling sorry for her. Poor, thin, sexy Sydney, spending all her time on the treadmill, trying to keep the pounds and the years at bay. I knew from personal experience that skinny fortysomethings didn't stay that way without daily effort and culinary denial. And for what? Like me and about every other woman I knew, Sydney was married, had a couple kids, and was surely seeing the big five-oh on the near horizon. Was that it? Fifty and "still hot" was another ideal that we needed to achieve. For whom? The guys? Her husband, my husband, the teens' MILF status? No matter what she did, there would come a time when it just wouldn't matter. She'd be skinny and old. Every mare gets put out to pasture. It just takes some getting used to.

My soup classes sold out.

"Soup is very popular," the director told me when I dropped off my winter class descriptions in December. She was right. Who doesn't like soup?

Soup has a storied history and a bright future. With a bowl of something steaming in hand, a crackling fire, and a good book, we can fight off the darkest winter night. And soup is every girl's dietary friend. There is volume and heat, and soup does fill us up—for half an hour, anyway. Soup carries the mantle of something Spartan and righteous. "I'll just have the soup" speaks of nobility. At Mescolanza, I was often amazed when someone ordered the soup, when there were so many other wonderful things to choose.

"What's the soup tonight?" a regular customer would ask.

"Minestrone," I would reply cheerfully. Minestrone was the one and only soup we ever made in the entire eleven years that we were open for business.

"I'll have the minestrone!" Yucks all around!

I put those soup people in the category of folks who were rabid about leash laws and went to town-planning council meetings religiously. If a character in one of my stories ate soup, he was probably a pill. I mean, I liked soup as much as the next gal, but I realized that I felt conflicted about it, or maybe just about soup eaters. Sydney probably ate a cup of vegetable soup when she was being naughty. Soup spoke to me of more contradictions: denial and nourishment. It's the food of nuns and prisoners, but it's also the life-affirming stuff of lobster boatmen and rugged pickpocketing orphans. It fuels both the constricted and the robust.

On class day I whipped up a short pot of *pastina* as my ladies chatted about getting back to their nonholiday schedules. I passed out ramekins full of the custardy soup to my ladies as a teaser of what was to come. Instantly, everyone felt taken care of. Chicken broth with pasta and egg does that to a person. As I set up the ingredients for the other soups, we spooned in the *pastina*'s warmth, and I could feel the comfort level rise. Conversations picked up. Mostly my students were recapping their holiday stories, but peppering the travelogues, like chili flakes meant to give *linguine vongole* a little charge, was the *d*-word. Lots of diet talk was going down.

"Oh, my sweet Lord, this is so good," Glenda exclaimed. "This is the best thing I've eaten since New Year's Day."

"It's the *only* thing she's eaten since New Year's Day," Tanya informed us, "unless you count the grapefruits."

"Not all of us are naturally skinny," Glenda shot back at her.

"I always start my diet right after Christmas," one of the new girls offered. "It's that week between Christmas and New Year's that's the killer."

"What diet are you on?"

That question sure was a January party-starter. Everybody except Tanya was on some kind of diet. And as different as each of the diets appeared to be, they all shared one very obvious component: denial.

"I just stay away from anything white."

"No animal products of any kind."

"Eliminate all sugars."

"Juice fast."

"Six times a day, never eat more than you can hold in your palm of your hand."

"Only mineral water with apple cider vinegar until the afternoon, then a half a banana at two o'clock, then a small bowl of brown rice at six o'clock, and that's it for two weeks."

I knew I needed to steer *(moo-ve)* this conversation into another field, as this was an Italian-cooking class and these ladies had signed up for some eating. Apparently, they were making exceptions to their diets, because they all wolfed down the *pastina*. These poor girls were starving! They needed some sustenance, and I was happy to give it to them.

When they finished eating, I divided them into meatball makers and vegetable choppers. We had soup pots bubbling on the stove. The rich steam from the beef broth perfumed the kitchen with a manly scent. We made dozens of tiny meatballs from grass-fed local beef, Italian parsley, garlic, whole-wheat bread crumbs, and parmigiana. I had to keep an eye on the meatball rollers, though—they were ignoring my instructions about what size to make the balls ("hazelnuts, ladies, not walnuts"). I knew it wasn't on purpose, but the little meatballs were morphing into large meatballs. *Things have a way of doing that,* I thought as I took one of Glenda's "I can't help it, I'm from Texas!" massive creations and divided in into thirds. "We want these *pallottoline* to be able to fit on our soupspoons," I reminded them.

We finished the class with an easy pumpkin custard that tastes like a soupy version of pumpkin pie without the crust. I topped each wet pudding with a plop of whipped Point Reyes cream sweetened with a pinch of sugar and a splash of amaretto. We sipped espresso as our time together wound down.

This was getting easier and easier. Glenda and Tanya were there—truly, they were my star students—and the other ladies seemed to come in pairs or small groups, too, so the noise level was substantial. And I liked that. During the class everyone was talking, rolling meatballs, chopping vegetables, and drinking their morning wine. This class was more of a show-and-tell for me, even with three soups and a dessert.

January is touted as a firecracker month of fresh starts, but actually it's a month for settling in and waiting. For the most part, January offers a break from the senior-year grind of deadlines and the all-consuming application process, unless your senior applied early decision to a fabulous university and got the gift of a "yes!"

So, that was that. Another class created and executed, and now even this exciting undertaking was morphing into something commonplace. I still had the necessary performance anxiety and nerves that every show-woman needs to come alive, but it sure didn't last very long. I found myself back in ho-hum mode within thirty minutes after my greeting and overview. The ladies left seemingly happy enough, headed off to do the same things they always did, I imagined. The same things I always did. I was feeling a shudder of resignation at the thought of another night of family and the demands that would come my way.

January is touted as a firecracker month of fresh starts, but actually it's a month for settling in and waiting. For the most part,

January offers a break from the senior-year grind of deadlines and the all-consuming application process, unless your senior applied early decision to a fabulous university and got the gift of a "yes!" In that case, look out. She may be ready to *paaarrr-ty!* The work is done, she's in, and who cares if her second-semester GPA is less than stellar? We know who cares. You do. This letting go of her work ethic is like the gateway drug to your bad motherhood. If you let up on the nagging, what will become of her? Perhaps you've heard that colleges look at admitted students' second-semester transcripts and change their mind if the grades have slipped. You've also heard stories about people waking up in bathtubs full of ice with a kidney missing, but do you really know anybody that's happened to?

On the other hand, maybe your senior—and, more important, you—will be dealing with the first rejection. You'll be telling yourself, *It's fine—it was only early decision. A reach anyway. Doesn't really mean anything.* And it doesn't, except when you run into another mom who knows the certainty of where her boy will be next year and you need to offer a heartfelt "Congratulations!" when you feel as if her kid got in only because of that damn crew you tried to convince your son to do but that he thought was too "gay"—the word he uses for anything you think is interesting. And now look who's going to Stanford (and who's not), and how *not* gay is that? Damn! If only you could've rowed that boat for him.

So here you are, stuck with a situation that makes you feel powerless, and there is only one thing you can do. Pick on yourself. The first and most immediate target is your body. And what better month to "just do it" than January? Everywhere you look, articles and advertisements are extolling the Puritan virtues of hard work and denial. Join a gym, clean your closets, tighten your budget, and—the number-one resolution on everybody's list—lose some weight. The multibillion-dollar weight-loss industry in this country thrives in all economic cycles, and for women especially, that means the *d*-word: "diet." This cursed word is associated with punishment, sitting on the sidelines, and suffering all alone. Let this be the first January you stop doing that.

Anyway, you've got better things to do. You've got comfort to give. Somebody needs you this January, and it's not who you think it is.

Maybe you're getting glimpses that life after the Goodbye Year won't be so bad after all. You're enjoying visions of your child healthy, happy, and settled in at the college of her choice. Not that you would take credit for her success, but it does feel good to know that you may have played some small part in her laudable accomplishment.

However, if launching your child into the world of university life defines motherhood success, then what designation do we give to the mother of a first-semester flunk-out? *Failure.* One frustrated, sad fellow mom.

We moms of a certain age have found ourselves thrust onto the competitive playing field of good mom versus bad mom. Bad moms are what most of our mothers were. Feed, clothe, shelter, and send Sally off to school. That's it—today's bad mom. Good moms make sure that Johnny's backpack is organized with his carefully edited (by her!) history paper, freshly laundered PE shirt, a high-protein snack, and the one-inch binder that his Spanish teacher emailed *her* about. Oh, yes, we are not alone in the enabling. Teachers and counselors are in on it, too. Can't blame them. Dash off an email to Mom regarding Johnny's last

We moms of a certain age have found ourselves thrust onto the competitive playing field of good mom versus bad mom. Bad moms are what most of our mothers were. Feed, clothe, shelter, and send Sally off to school. That's it—today's bad mom. Good moms make sure that Johnny's backpack is organized with his carefully edited (by her!) history paper, freshly laundered PE shirt, a high-protein snack, and the one-inch binder that his Spanish teacher emailed *her* about. For the moms who try to do everything they can to help Sally and Johnny along, are there trophies or medals? No, there is just a pejorative: "Helicopter Mom."

poor test score, and she's on it. Remind Mom that the algebra midterm is in two days, and now somehow she's on the hook for the test, too. So, for the moms who try to do everything they can to help Sally and Johnny along, are there trophies or medals? No, there is just a pejorative: "Helicopter Mom."

I bucked that trend when my children were young. Having babies who turned into little kids just seemed like the most natural thing in the world to me. Clearly, I was a throwback to a mid-twentieth-century mom. It did not occur to me to read a book on how to engage my children. I loved them. Our life together engaged them. I didn't understand the new style of parenting that was taking over my peers. I felt bad for them. My mom friends were so anxious, worried about everything from the first-grade curriculum to the games at recess. I listened to them and saw that they were doing the same thing I was—loving their kids—but we were going about it a little differently. Again, it's not like I invented my style of parenting. My kids heard a lot of "Sure, okay, sounds like fun," but "no" wasn't a foreign word. The classic "because I said so" was respected as the final final. I just copied what I knew. It worked.

And based on what I was observing around me—the twenty-minute end-of-playdate negotiations moms were having with their youngsters to get them to put on a jacket and head out the door—this new system wasn't very appetizing. Anyway, I was too busy with the restaurant to be concerned with all the little details, but mostly because the attendant hovering was boring to me. When I'd pick up one of my kids from a visit, the mom would tell me about all the things they (she included) had done. Souvenirs—cupcakes, crafts—of their time together would often accompany this report. From my perspective, it looked like the biggest pain in the ass. Wasn't the whole idea of a playdate that it was a time when young pals could be together and do what kids do? By themselves? The kids could play and the mom would be there to keep it legal, offering refreshments and the occasional Band-Aid. I noticed that the hovered kids, for the most part, were kinda miserable to be around. They'd come for an after-school visit and look to me to entertain them.

I didn't live in a vacuum, so, of course, I learned some of the buzzwords. We had a lot of "parallel play." We played "let's go to the bank, the post office, the market, and the printer to pick up the new menus, and you guys can put coins in the meter!" We went to the park sometimes, but it seemed like all the other kids were having playdates with their moms. My model was moms talking (smoking cigarettes), kids playing. Mommy and Me? I lived with them. We saw a lot of each other.

They attended a first-rate school, and when the wave of enrichment programs started to build, I fleetingly thought I should enroll them in some things. But like me during my childhood, after spending hours cooped up in the classroom, they just wanted to go outside and play. It got to the point where they knew their playmates' schedules, which days they were free.

"No, Gordon can't come over. He has fencing today."

"What about Billy?"

"Chess and then Japanese tutor. But he can come over tomorrow after violin."

"You guys want to take chess?"

"*No!*"

They could take, but mostly leave, video games. They didn't care about that stuff. They certainly weren't overscheduled with lessons. I was the opposite of the Tiger Mom. I was Sea Otter Mom. But make no mistake about that—I was Boss Sea Otter. A controlling Boss Sea Otter Mom. It felt right and safe to just allow them to be kids, so I didn't do any hovering, although I did have clear lines of what was okay with me, which boxed them in. But it was a pretty big box, and inside it they could do whatever they wanted. I bought them dry ice, we launched rockets. We biked together, they biked by themselves, they helped me in the garden, they played a lot of Wiffle ball (sometimes with me pitching), watched TV (gasp!), and had a good time.

It's not hard for me to pull out a moment from my vault of memories of early motherhood. I had three babies in the span of fewer than five years. I can hear their toddler giggles, I can taste their wet kisses, and I can see me playing the fun mommy. My husband was the rule maker; I was the rule breaker. I loved that role. I remember a day at the beach I'd spent with two friends and their children. The fog had burned off and the afternoon was golden. My children splashed in the waves, dug in the sand, and collected offerings from the sea. I gave them more freedom than other mothers afforded their kids. As the sun started to pull away from us, Page was at my side.

"Come on, boys," I called out to my eight- and nine-year-old sons. "Time to go."

They picked up their pails and shovels and made their way to our blanket. My girlfriends' jaws dropped simultaneously.

"They just listen to you?" one marveled.

"How do you do that?" asked the other. "It will take me an hour to get my kids off this beach."

I was pleased with myself. I had this parenting thing down. Here was the proof. They listened to me, which made them easy, which made for a lot of fun. Surprising them with tea-party dinners, stretching out their bedtimes, and granting them extra privileges whenever the whim of my powerful benevolence struck was my specialty. I thought I was being a fantastic parent, but now I know that it was something else. I was like the exciting older friend who had the stuff that fascinated them. They would do whatever it took to stay in my orbit and good graces.

By the time Page was a senior, my preternatural parenting confidence was slipping. The demon voices found my *you are not doing a good job* spot. And they went to town. Maybe the Tiger Moms were right. You had to push your kids. Hover around, demand excellence, and sign them up for Mathletes whether they liked it or not. Make the most of their time. Trouble was, I was the shits at time management. I was happy that Page was so self-disciplined, which for a while left me off the hook. But now, with only months to go before her future would be decided, I was really worried that all the work she had done in high school wouldn't stack up against the resumes of the kids whose moms had enriched their lives with concrete activities instead of "Let's go to a baseball game!"

This January might be the first time you notice the fallout from last year's matriculating class of college freshmen raised by Helicopter Moms: the Boomerang Kids. You'll see them bagging groceries or working at the coffee shop. More than once, I have put my foot in my mouth by asking with irritating good cheer, "Michael, when are you going back?" only to realize a few beats too late that it's well past the start date of a second semester. One of Page's classmates, a brilliant student, hated the freshman experience so much that she opted not to return to her coveted college after Thanksgiving break. Her parents had her stuff shipped back, and after a semester off, she enrolled at a local art school, where she is thriving. *Living at home* and thriving. The kids are elastic, and this turnabout for them is just another stop on their youthful journey. Ah, but for the moms, it's another story.

Maybe it's your sister-in-law or a neighbor who is hurting this January. Aside from the fact that her newly claimed craft room is back to being a teen bedroom, she is feeling that as a mother she has come up short. All the essay coaches, the teacher meetings, the intense focus that she made her mission for the last four years (ha—more like eighteen) have been for naught. Whether her child flunked out or simply couldn't function without her constant prodding and total availability, the result is the same: He is sprawled on the couch at home, relieved that he is no longer struggling with something he may not have wanted in the first place, and casually considering his options. Mom is there beside him, wondering what went wrong (translation: what she did wrong) and feeling like crap.

She needs a hug and a bowl of soup.

Make a double batch and make a date (don't take no for an answer) with a mom you know who is adjusting to the return of her beloved child. She's got it all bottled up inside. I bet if you allow her to tell her story, she will *hear* it, too. And in that telling she will realize not only that it is not the end of the world, but also that there is no reason for blame to be part of the story. Not for her son, and especially not for her.

When my friend Sari's twin daughters won a public-service award for their work with a local food bank, Sari deflected any compliments that came her way. "I had nothing to do with it," she would respond when friends congratulated her on the values that she must have instilled in her daughters. But when the young ladies got caught shoplifting, Sari accepted responsibility

Sometimes we just have to sit with the "what ifs," not resisting, but allowing our female wisdom to rise to the surface. Don't fall prey to the marketing of "just do it" this January. Be quiet so you can hear what your spirit is trying to tell you. Question the negative voices. Put them in the hot seat. When they start in on you with their needling, jabbing criticism, stop and ask, *Who in the hell is talking to me?* It's not You, because if it were You, she wouldn't be picking on you.

for the act as if she had slipped the matching pairs of designer sunglasses into her own purse.

Do all mothers do this? I don't know. I do know that I have felt the same way Sari did. Our children do something good, and it is all them; they screw up, and it must be our fault. We gave too much/too little. We were too strict/too lenient. We were too busy with our own careers to notice that they were in great need. We were too involved in their everyday, and we have handicapped them for all eternity. This is the proverbial no-win situation. Like that rascal Captain Kirk, I don't believe in a no-win situation.

Sometimes we just have to sit with the "what ifs," not resisting, but allowing our female wisdom to rise to the surface. Don't fall prey to the marketing of "just do it" this January. Be quiet so you can hear what your spirit is trying to tell you. Question the negative voices. Put them in the hot seat. When they start in on you with their needling, jabbing criticism, stop and ask, *Who in the hell is talking to me?* It's not You, because if it were You, she wouldn't be picking on you.

Most important, enjoy the simple calm and comfort of being there for a friend, taking it all in, and celebrating the deep winter silence with the knowledge that the nights are, ever so slightly, giving way to longer days.

♡ THE RECIPE

. . . .

Pastina

Pastina is the remedy for a cold, the remedy for the feeling that you might be getting a cold, and the remedy for the ill-formed wish that you had a cold so you could stay in bed with a book and ignore the laundry. *Pastina* is the perfect dish to prepare when you come home from work wet and tired and don't want to go out. *Pastina* makes the fastest bowl of comfort to soothe a broken heart. I've fed it to the boys when they've lost a play-off game, I've fed it to Page when she didn't even get honorable mention at the speech contest (both years), and I've eaten bowls of it when I didn't know what to do with myself.

The essential ingredients are three. Seriously, just three. So you have to make sure they are the best three you can find. One: *il brodo*, the broth. If you can make your own, you will always crave that flavor when you think of chicken broth, but come on—who has time to be boiling up a vat of it every other day? Sure, tossing the ingredients into the big stockpot is a no-brainer: chicken bones and skin, necks and wings, celery, carrot, onion, and parsley. But then you have to cool it, skim off the fat, strain it, pour it into storage containers, and clean up the greasy mess. There are rewards for this work. It is easy to sleep at night when you know that you have a cache of frozen broth in your basement deep freeze. But if you're not on the peppy pills, the good news is that you can buy broth from the grocery store. Look for the organic free-range kind. Two: the pasta. So simple—buy De Cecco or Barilla pastina. Or Eduardo's *stellette*. Three: the eggs. Collect them from the nests of your backyard flock of Anconas and Leghorns. Okay, buy local, free-range ones. Just don't buy the white ones that come from the saddest locked-up chickens on the planet because they cost ten cents. They aren't even worth the ten cents, but you and your loved ones are worth a wholesome, creamy bowl of *pastina* any day of the week.

What You Need

1 quart chicken broth

About 8 ounces any tiny cut of pasta

3 eggs

INSTRUCTIONS

Pour the broth in a large saucepan and heat to boiling. Add the pasta; cook for about 6 minutes, then lower the heat to the lowest setting.

Whip up three beautiful yellow-yolked whole eggs short of a froth. Gently fold the eggs into the hot mix with a wide spatula. This will yield a custardy-pasta-chickeny-tasting pot of goodness. If you are feeling frisky, crack some green and black peppercorns or add some freshly grated parmigiana on top of each steaming bowl.

 January

The last thing you need is to beat yourself up because your body took on a few extra pounds. Make *pastina* and nourish yourself. Be nice to you, thank your body for taking you places, and just take it easy. January is a fallow, dark month, and all those "just do it" resolution lists are merely devices to make you feel bad and join a sweaty health club. Don't give them your money. Spend it on a massage or a pedicure. Take a walk. Drink water with sliced cucumber. Take care of yourself, and trust me, you'll soon be peeing the unwanted pounds right down the drain.

✓ To Do: *Give Name and Face to Your Bullies*
This is a fun exercise that has many names but ultimately rewards you with clarity and empowering detachment. Some coaches call them saboteurs. Psychologists refer to the voice as the superego. These recriminating voices all share only one goal: to keep you stuck in the exact place you are. I like to call

them bullies, because if you know a bully, he is nothing more than a coward. Change is threatening to these bullies. When you hear the negative voice, stop and try to imagine what he or she looks like. I found that during my Goodbye Year, I had two constant companions, who slunk around my ankles like Ursula's Flotsam and Jetsam in *The Little Mermaid*. They were great bullies, because they were smart, which appealed to my vanity. And they were elastic. Sometimes they'd play Good Demon/Bad Demon. They were sarcastic and witty as they put me down and planted seeds of doubt about every aspect of my motherhood.

The great value of the exercise is that once we flesh out our bullies, they become something that exists outside our true selves. For a while, they'll stick around like annoying mosquitoes, but what will be different will be that when they start up, you will recognize them—*Oh, you two again!*—as the tedious nothings that they are. And one day soon, they'll just buzz off.

6 · The Weight of Love

FEBRUARY
RECIPE: *Zabaglione Perfetto*

"Did you hear about Whitney's Bob?" Tabitha asked me, as we finished the last of the dishes we had used to serve the lunch from my February cooking class. Whitney was married to a Bob. So were Tabitha, Melanie, and half a dozen other ladies in town. The husband Bobs were identified (naturally) by their wife's first name.

"Melanie saw him at MarketBar at the Ferry Plaza with some woman, and she said that he seemed flustered when she said hello." Tabitha continued, "Then, when she was leaving, she saw them sitting closer together and having a second bottle of wine."

I didn't know Whitney that well, and I sure as heck didn't care about her Bob. Not that I knew anything about the daytime activities of those investment-banker guys, but I imagined that they had expensive bottles of wine with their clients every day—though I had an inkling of where Tabitha was going with this.

"I don't think Whitney has anything to worry about. She was probably just an old friend."

"Oh, she was an old friend, all right," Tabitha said, as she snapped off her pink polka-dot latex gloves. "She was his high school girlfriend, and he's moved into a South Beach condo with her."

"What an ass!" I'd never liked that Bob.

My mind flashed on the faces of their two adorable children.

"How could he leave those kids?" I asked Tabitha. It wasn't really a question.

"I know," she offered in understanding.

How could he leave those kids? was the first thought that came to my mind. Why wasn't it *How could he leave Whitney?*

Because that wasn't too much of a quandary. During my third Goodbye Year, I didn't know of any long-term partnership (mine included) that wasn't a little strained. If you have teenagers, you've probably been together long enough to take each other for granted at the very least, or harbor some loathsome feelings for each other at the worst.

And hey, Valentine, how's your sex life?

Uh-huh.

He moves my car again. I never move his car, because it's his car. My car is the "family" car, which places it in the community-property slush pile of our long-married lives. I don't have the keys to his car. I don't want them. During the carting-the-kids-around years, I envied him his car, void of the detritus of mom life. Now, with them all driving off—in their own cars—I've laid claim to mine. The Trooper is my car. Still, he moves it from the spot where I have parked it; he adjusts the rearview mirror to his height. And he does this because I know (though he'll deny it) that he thinks it is our car. The one I use. My clothes are my clothes, but even my bike is somehow his to lend to a friend.

"Where are you going with my bike?" I ask him when I see it

attached to the back of his car. He's says he's taking it to a friend's house so they can ride together.

"Why does it have to be my bike?" I protest in the form of a question. Page's bike still resides here. He exhales with the force of a blow in my direction.

"I maintain it," he says, like that gives him ownership. I maintain the contents of the refrigerator and the pantry, but my service doesn't give me ownership. His does.

I wasn't planning on going on a ride, and it's not like the bike will get used up, and the friend who will pedal my bike is dear to me, and yet . . . the body memory, like an accessible raw nerve, pings and rushes up from my feet to my stomach to my mouth, and I bark, *Even though I can't eat the hay, I don't want the horses and donkey to eat it.* This is what I've become: The Dog in the Manger. Mean and small.

I know this isn't about my bike or my car. It's about the breakdown of boundaries, borders that have eroded from the steady rain of years of marriage. We stand in the garage. Silence. I tear at the cuticle on the middle finger of my right hand. It hurts. It hurts that the good feelings of the long weekend, the food, the wine, the sex—the bike rides!—are trashed now because we have landed in the well-worn groove of the record of our lives together.

He says "goodbye" solidly, unmistakably, like a hang-up on a rotary-dial desk phone. I am left alone to stew in the rancid soup I have made of our relationship. No, he's not off the hook. He's been here all along, pretending with me. But he will return and things will thaw, and we will share a meal together, and tomorrow will be another day of the marriage we are both afraid to examine out loud.

My first personal music system was a record player with a spindle that could play both 33s (the records of my parents' generation) and (with a plastic adapter) larger-holed 45s. The ninety-nine-cent iRecord of the sixties was the 45 single, affordable to twelve-year-old babysitters. My collection consisted of six records, the Beatles being the best value because chances were, the flip side was going to have a song I liked, even a hit. I played them over and over, and eventually all this use would cause a skip to happen, a place where the needle got stuck.

There were ways to fix this. You could tape a penny on the arm of the record player, and the extra weight would force the needle to jump over the skip. You might miss a beat or two, but you still had the song. And most of it was just fine. But ultimately, the record would develop another bump, a scratch, a sticky spot, and then it would become just not worth listening to that song, your favorite song, with the predictable jarring disturbances. I hung on to scratched and irritating records long after playing them was joyful. I hung on to them because they still had value to me. And it was all the music I had.

The history of love: One plus one equals two that magically turn into one. You can't get enough of each other. Where does one leave off and the other begin? Who cares! It's so wonderful to be in love. You love your parents, your country, your dog . . . but oh, to be *in* love. Electricity at the touch. Sex, Sex, Sex! There's just so much love in surplus that you have to make something of it or you will burst. A baby. Bliss. Love has reached a new level. Now, one plus one equals three and an abundance of joy. Your connection goes deeper. You've made something that is, will always be, a part of both of you. But—and here's the thing that is a slippery snake—there's an almost imperceptible shift.

You, Mom, are so full of love and hormones, you don't even notice. Your identity has taken on a new nuance—mother. You welcome this addition, this expansion, this delicious complexity to the You of you. You understand that the demands of mothering need to take center stage; he understands that, too. Kinda.

I confess (and have heard my pals confess this countless times) that there were years when sex at the end of a busy day was just *one more thing* that *I* had to do before I could fall asleep. Pathetic but true. Why does that happen? Was it that long ago that we couldn't keep our hands off each other? Yes, after the birth of your first child, it might as well have been a lifetime ago. And by the time he or she reaches senior year . . .

If you asked him, the biggest problem in our relationship would be lack of sex. If you asked me, I'd suggest we sit down for a cup of coffee and I'd pull out my laundry list of problems, subproblems, and overreaching problems. We tried therapy for a while. It was like trying an introductory gym membership.

"Oh, this is great! I'm going to work out all the time, at least four times a week," I'd say after my first sweaty Zumba class. The optimism from Dr. Livingston—"Your relationship can be anything you want it to be"—felt like that. I should have known better from past experiences with dropping the ball, but I believed this shift in our priorities (taking the time and effort to right the relationship ship) would get us to and keep us working out at the marital gym. We'd be taking care of ourselves, and the therapy would take care of our relationship. If only it were that easy. Just put your mind to the task and fix it. Right? Determination is the American way. But for hubby and me, just like our waned enthusiasm for the Stairmaster, the metaphorical free month expired, and that was that.

I was taping a penny on the phonograph arm again, hoping to skip over the scratches that came from years of wear. Dr. L suggested we remember what it felt like when we first discovered our passion for each other. It's elusive.

I remember catching my breath midsentence because his fingers were dancing on my knee under the table at one of our first holiday dinners with his family. I remember the warmth of twenty loaves of fresh bread picked up for the restaurant that filled his sports car with the aroma of desire. His thigh taut, sliding the gearshift into third to accommodate both of us in the driver's seat. Stolen kisses in a walk-in filled with garbage bags full of basil. A temporarily abandoned mound of gnocchi on the pantry table beside two empty bottles of beer. Quickies. Shots of sexual adrenaline. Spontaneity and the feeling that everything was possible. Where did that go?

Later, there were Christmas Eves when the kids were all tucked in and the lovemaking was pure contentment. We made love to each other and to our life. The joy of loving them filled us up, and slowly loving them took the place of loving each other. So busy in those years, we'd wrangle the occasional night away from the restaurant and the three kids to go out to dinner. And what would we talk about? We'd talk about them. Our all-encompassing love for the three little hearts that loved us back without conditions. And that love for them, individually and collectively, changed us.

Think about it. Do you know of any long-term marriages (love affairs) that have kept that intensity alive? Married couples with teenage children? Teens who are experiencing sexual excitement for themselves? Really? You know some sexually hot-for-each-other parents of good-looking, hard-bodied, wrinkleless children who are oozing sex? I want to meet these imaginary people.

Because what's happened, from the flash of time it took us to help Sally memorize her multiplication tables to our now-daily entreaties to Johnny to finish his senior essay, is that the kids have hijacked our sex lives. And for moms, the essence of who we are sexually has been buried like the skeleton in the family closet.

There is this raunchy Italian joke: Guido confesses to his priest that he is unfaithful in his marriage. The priest asks if he loves his wife and if they are having sexual relations. "Yes and yes," Guido answers, "but my mistress does things to me that my wife does not." Perhaps, offers the priest, if he asked her, his wife would do those things, too. Shocked, Guido replies, "Father! She kisses my son with those lips!"

Moms aren't supposed to have a sex life. When my nephew learned that his mom had read every word of the unholy trilogy of *Fifty Shades of Grey*, this successful thirty-year-old turned back into the little boy I knew. "Mom! Why did you tell me? I don't want to know that!" he exclaimed, middle-school inflection of "what is *yuck*" in every word, as he repeated his part of this disturbing conversation he had had with my sister-in-law.

"Your mom is a sensual woman," I told him, as he made faces like he had just gotten a mouthful of sour milk. I've known her since high school, when she and my brother started dating. But my nephew wants to see her only as Mom, an entity of undying maternal love and devotion, not as someone of the same species as the sexy women he dates.

I get it. We wear masks for our children. When they are little, we protect them from our adult troubles (and adult fun) in our noble desire to keep their childhoods innocent. But the trouble

We wear masks for our children. When they are little, we protect them from our adult troubles (and adult fun) in our noble desire to keep their childhoods innocent. But the trouble is we, Hubby and Wife, get so used to those masks that we just keep wearing them when they no longer serve a purpose.

is we, Hubby and Wife, get so used to those masks that we just keep wearing them when they no longer serve a purpose. Unless the purpose of the mask serves as a shield to our authenticity. Why would we want a shield? Because we are afraid that if we show each other who we really are, we won't like us anymore.

Beyond the fact that Hubby and I had become creatures of habit, we had, more important, become creatures of habitat. Food and *What will I make for dinner?* defined my day. The nightly communion of my familiar cuisine and school stories from the three kids was a check-in that cemented the relationships the five of us shared. Even after our core shrunk from five to four to three to just the two of us, I kept cooking the same quantities.

There was always room at our table for friends who stopped by for a glass of wine. In the nest that I kept feathered and warm, with sports on the television, open-house dinners, and Rolling Rock—same as it ever was—role playing was a powerful magnet holding Jeff and me in place. As each child left for college, I dug in deeper and held on tighter to what felt like all that was left of our marriage.

Dinner.

Like my Italian aunties, I think about what I'll make for dinner when I'm having my morning cappuccino. The market inspires me, but I'm not surprised when I get there and find apricots in late May or persimmons in early November. A childhood connection to the garden and the seasons is as much a part of me as the color of my eyes. I know the local/seasonal banner has turned what poor rural folks used to eat into an elite foodie manifesto. Ironically, my family and friends from the hamlet I grew up in now eat food from China. Not Chinese food, but food from China, Australia, Zimbabwe—wherever the megaconvenience stores source their two-dollar hamburgers. The family dairy farms are gone, the cornfields covered in asphalt to hold the cars that fill up on petroleum while the drivers fill up on fast food that has traveled countless miles.

It's sad to witness what has become of my pastoral Pennsylvania childhood home, but there are pockets of imagination starting to coalesce. A farmers' market here, a natural butcher there. What my generation took for granted disappeared from the next in the name of time management. Moms were working outside the home, and the old model of domestic arts was replaced with a welcomed second paycheck. No doubt growing, cooking, canning, baking was a second full-time job (second to the mom role) for my mom, aunts, and neighbors. Maybe all that daily work is what made the mothering less anxious. They were too freaking busy to worry about whether the fourth-grade history curriculum should include the French Revolution. Or maybe the fresh food made everybody calmer. As a kid, I knew that what the moms did was a service in the name of love, and—here's that question again—why did/do I think that? Is love service? It has felt like that to me.

We naturally serve our children. We take care of things for them. We do their laundry; some of us even do their homework! And what about our spouses? Does our service turn us into servants? Do we strike a silent bargain to get what we want, which is maintaining the comfort of the status quo, by giving them what they want? Genuine service, doing something for a loved one, comes from the heart space and feels good. It feels like love to me to shop for the food, make the dinner, serve the dinner, and delight my family. But if the service we perform is motivated by fear of our loved ones' negative reaction if we don't do it, that is not love.

I have been very popular with my kids. I knew what to do to maintain my status, and I held up my end of our silent bargain. For years, I was afraid of losing that popularity. But the price of people-pleasing—even if, or maybe especially if, those people were my kids and husband—just got too steep. That's why I was so sad. I had created a persona that I made bargains with. *I don't want to do that thing, but if I don't do that thing, they'll be disappointed in me and take their love away, so I'll just do that thing.* Compromise sounds like taking the high road in the service of relationships, but the flip side of that coin is the kind of compromise that shames us: We devalue who we are in the act of making the concessions that keep us in the same familiar place. It's cowardly.

> Compromise sounds like taking the high road
> in the service of relationships, but the flip side
> of that coin is the kind of compromise that
> shames us: We devalue who we are in the act
> of making the concessions that keep us in the
> same familiar place.

Maybe you have already gone through the pain/joy of divorce. Maybe you have found another lover. Or maybe you are just going through the motions of a relationship because the thought of anything else is terrifying. So, to hold those fear-based emotions at arm's length, you keep feeding yourself big bites of BS, numbing yourself into a passionless existence, justifying the status with ridiculous isms. *This is just the way it is after X years of marriage. No relationship stays the way it was in the beginning. Sex just isn't that important anymore.* Yeah, right! Just ask Whitney's Bob or any of the Toms, Dicks, or Harrys you know who have walked out on a long-term partnership if sex isn't that important.

Your intimate relationship has been caught up in the vortex of energy that is the business of your family. Fulfilling the demands of mothering the ship requires you to spin with such power that the centrifugal force alone has sustained things. As the final buoy of your child's senior year of high school floats into view, you will be able to catch a glimpse of the schism that his splintering-off will cause. You have got to look this tornado right in the eye, ladies. It may feel like all the plates you have kept aloft are going to come crashing down. Some surely will. But it doesn't have to end with regrets and resignation. And it doesn't have to end in divorce.

Dr. L told us, "You can make your relationship anything you want it to be." Well, Bibbidi-Bobbidi-Boo! I embraced that statement as a beautiful fantasy, but not a fantasy as in, *It's a fantasy. Never gonna happen.* No, I embraced it like, *Miracles happen every day!* I am a believer in fairy tales. I expected it—our connected, loving, sex-on-wheels relationship would just rematerialize, fueled by the power of wanting and hoping. Close my eyes, click my heels, make it better. Get us home to the fire of what brought us together in the first place. I realize now that the knocking I heard during my first Goodbye Year was a growth opportunity. As much as I wanted to ignore it, it was as persistent as a salesman at the door of the next phase of my life, challenging me to examine my beliefs around this nebulous thing called our marriage.

Over the years, I had started focusing on it like it was outside me, a third-party proxy to my life. When each Last Time, each inevitable moment of *she won't be here next year* arrived— *Remember how long she wore that* Little Mermaid *costume I made for her? We had to put Band-Aids on her fin when we took her trick-or-treating because it was covered with boo-boos*—I felt like another hole was forming in my heart. I looked to my husband to fill it. No, more accurately, I looked to our relationship to take up the space her leaving was creating.

There was my life, Hubby's life, and the beast in the room, our relationship. And because I (like you, dear reader), the universal mom, end up caring for all of the animals that inhabit my life, I took over caring for the beast. I wanted to make the beast happy. I thought that was in my power. I'd feed the beast with three-course dinners, entertain him with domestic arts. I'd groom the beast by pleasing him with a beautiful and inviting home. I'd try to make the beast proud by looking good. But you know what? Nothing would satisfy that beast for any length of time. When you put your energy into caring for something, and nothing you are doing works, it's depressing. You gain the weight of your unappreciated efforts. You try to ignore the bastard by stepping around his ever-growing mass with television, wine, exercise, PTA. But the beast is still there. Until he's not.

Truth was, I was afraid if the beast got mad, he'd ditch me just like Whitney's Bob ditched her. That beast that I was so afraid of angering was just a paper tiger after all.

How could he leave those kids? Weren't they the insurance policy we bought and paid for with our sacrifices on the sexual altar? Isn't it the great nobility of parents to "stay together for the sake of the kids"? You want that carved on your matching tombstones? *They took their marriage to the grave, but at least they didn't complicate their children's lives with a break-up.* How dare Bob reach for some personal happiness at the expense of his "happy" home life? How dare he, indeed!

It takes courage to live with your heart. I'm just going to say it again here, girls. Courage. *Coeur*, French for "heart," that's the root of the word. In my experience, it's more often the guys who take heart (and take the leap of faith into another's arms) than the women—quite a contradiction of the standard definitions of the male and female psyche. We're supposed to be the

The word "vulnerable" might conjure up helplessness or susceptibility to attack, but allowing yourself to be vulnerable opens up a part of you that says, *I'm willing to take this leap*. Inherent in risk is courage. You know what the opposite of that feels like. At the heart of vulnerability beats a feeling of self-worth. I think men are better at holding on to that feeling than we are.

emotional ones. Maybe it's because they are wired in a more singular straight line. Maybe it's because they are pricks. I think it's because they allow themselves to be vulnerable—a risky place to live, but what an alive place it is. The word "vulnerable" might conjure up helplessness or susceptibility to attack, but allowing yourself to be vulnerable opens up a part of you that says, *I'm willing to take this leap*. Inherent in risk is courage. You know what the opposite of that feels like. At the heart of vulnerability beats a feeling of self-worth. I think men are better at holding on to that feeling than we are.

Moms, we are not measured by some yardstick. But every

You are worthy of love and happiness. The real
you with all the imperfections just like everybody
else. No doubt there have been years of external
pressures covering up the You of you, and we sure
are good at making nice. As the kids approach
their discovery of their own sexuality, it freaks
them out to picture Mom feeling or (God forbid!)
doing the things they are feeling and thinking
about doing. Well, too bad. Everybody needs to
grow this senior year.

image we see tells us that we are. We don't look like movie stars.
We don't look like we used to look. We don't look like the mom
next door. We moms of seniors certainly don't look like our
daughters or like our sons' girlfriends. So how can we be sexy?
How can we feel desirable when we compare ourselves to this
standard of beauty—no, not beauty, but modern-day "hotness"?
Don't we just love to pick on ourselves? Look in the mirror; see
the wrinkles, the bulges, the sags. I have never seen my husband
looking at his ass. 'Cause you know what? It doesn't matter what
his ass looks like in relation to how "sexy" he feels.

You are worthy of love and happiness. The real you with all the imperfections just like everybody else. No doubt there have been years of external pressures covering up the You of you, and we sure are good at making nice. As the kids approach their discovery of their own sexuality, it freaks them out to picture Mom feeling or (God forbid!) doing the things they are feeling and thinking about doing. Well, too bad. Everybody needs to grow this senior year. It's time for your beloved children to really see you, but before they can, you need to take a look in the mirror and admire the beautiful, sensual, loving woman that you are. Happy Valentine's Day!

♡ THE RECIPE

···

Zabaglione Perfetto (Creamy Egg Custard)

Praise God, the kids will be out of the house soon, which leaves more time for sex in the kitchen. Which leads us to our monthly recipe, perfect for an intimate Valentine's Day dessert for two— creamy, sweet, velvety, zabaglione.

WHAT YOU NEED

4 egg yolks
Ultra-fine sugar
Marsala wine
Berries or cherries
A copper round-bottomed pan (preferably one with a handle)

Instructions

What is sexier than a froth of warm zabaglione? Well, maybe what comes after. Start boiling some water. Separate 4 eggs, reserve the whites for another use, and save the best half egg-shell for measuring.

Tenderly place the 4 egg yolks in a copper bowl. Add 4 half shells' worth of sugar and 4 generous half shells' worth of Marsala wine.

Hold the bowl over the churning, hot, yearning water, but don't let it touch the surface. Tease the water.

Whip the yolks into a sweet frenzy till they almost reach a peak and you are almost spent. When the glow comes to your skin, spoon your creation over sweet berries and surrender.

 February

Love? No, sex. Remember that? That's what got you into this mess in the first place. Start to count how many days you make love this month. Paltry total? You hear of infidelities and divorce. You think of your old boyfriends. Your kids are having more sex than you are. Okay, don't think about that! For that matter, don't think about your kids at all this month of hearts and flowers. Think about how you're going to get your groove back!

✓ To Do: *Find Your Inner Venus*

Come on, she's in there somewhere. My Italian aunties never lost theirs. On the American scale of attractiveness, they probably wouldn't earn a three, but on the mysteriously sexy scale, they kick butt. What is it that they have going for them? They are comfortable in their own female skin, and they flaunt it. They aren't afraid to show that they have breasts. They wear form-fitting clothes. They wear high heels. Maybe these things don't work for you, but you've got to find something that does. Treat yourself to a new, skimpy nightie, something with spaghetti straps, or find a scent that turns you on, or read a hot romance. Cut your hair, color your hair, get a tattoo, take up pole dancing. (Or square dancing, which I think is very sexy, do-si-do.) Dig deep into the fecund soil of your girlie powers and unearth the lovely, sexy creature that you are. Get your hands dirty!

7 · Rejection

MARCH
RECIPE: *La Bagna Cauda*

As mothers, we instinctively give our babies what they want. They cry from hunger and we feed them. They want to be held and we pick them up. They want diversion and we read to them, we play with them, we buy them things. A relationship is formed. They want/need something and we provide it. We become the benevolent facilitators of their life, and in that process we lay claim to some of that life and (sorry, moms) give up some of ours. We can truly identify with only one life, and that is why their disappointments become our disappointments and hurt us so much. And as they get older and the slights and hurts go deeper, we get more lost.

How many times do you get together with a girlfriend for a cup of coffee and ask, "How are you?" and she responds with stories of what her children are doing? That is the barometer of how she is. If her kids are happy, she is sort of happy living through their accomplishments, but if her kids are unhappy, she is miserable. So modern moms get a knockoff version of joy if the kids are doing well and a virulent-swine-flu dose of melan-

How many times do you get together with a girlfriend for a cup of coffee and ask, "How are you?" and she responds with stories of what her children are doing? That is the barometer of how she is. If her kids are happy, she is sort of happy living through their accomplishments, but if her kids are unhappy, she is miserable. So modern moms get a knockoff version of joy if the kids are doing well and a virulent-swine-flu dose of melancholy if they are not. This doesn't sound like a life to me. But it was the one I was living.

choly if they are not. This doesn't sound like a life to me. But it was the one I was living.

Each time we let go of control of our children's lives, we gain a little of ours. And let's face it, girls, "control" is a loaded word. I used to think that I could control every external in my children's lives. I found evidence of that belief when they were infants. But as soon as they were out of my controlling force field, they were susceptible to the world and to experiences that I could not control. It's not like we moms are evil dictators; we are the protectors of our children's hearts and we will do anything to keep them from hurt. But just as was true for Sleeping Beauty, even if we burn all the spinning wheels in the kingdom, she will still get nicked on that spindle.

I was unprepared for the zing of my daughter's flesh when the spinning wheel's spindle pierced it.

It was Saint Patrick's Day, and I was getting dressed for a party. I had one green eyelash stuck to my eyelid and was in the process of gluing on the other one when it happened to me. My daughter might argue that it happened to *her*, but that's her story. Every mother I know knows that This is about us.

"I didn't get in," she said on the phone. Our bedrooms were on opposite ends of the house, and though it is but a cottage, we were in the habit of calling each other. You know, for fun.

"What do you mean?" I was stalling because I couldn't recognize the emotion in her voice—Incredulity? Ironic disdain? Devastation?—and I was fussing with the placement of the second eyelash, which was becoming increasingly difficult with the phone cradled on my shoulder.

"I didn't get in to UCLA," she repeated to me with an emotion I did recognize—frustration bordering on anger because her mother was such a moron.

How could that be? Her grades and test scores were at the top of the charts.

Back in the day when Abe Lincoln and I were applying to colleges, there didn't seem to be much to it. You filled out the application and got accepted. These days, it's a stage of life. There's infancy, preschool, elementary school, and then platform building for the college application process, which lasts until acceptance. We're talking, like, six years!

When I look back on my daughter's youth, it seems way too short. Even before middle school she fell in with a tough crowd, the academic gang. I tried to steer her to the party girls, but you know they never like the friends you pick for them.

"I just found out online," she elaborated, and then added, "Hillary got in."

That news twisted like a Klingon batliff to the heart. The only thing worse than not being included in the in-crowd is finding out that your best friend is. And the only thing worse than *that* is wearing crooked green eyelashes to a party loaded with parents of high school seniors, hosted by the mother of successful Hillary, and leaving your loser daughter behind with a cold loaf of Irish soda bread.

Oh, these connections from your child's pain to your pain. There's really nothing like it, is there, Mom? The travel time is zip, and it arrives expanded, amplified, yet broken into tiny fragments like fireworks exploding under your skin. Your child's pain *is* your pain. You signed on for the transfer when you gave birth to her. Unavoidable, right? Or is there another way to love your child? Could this symbiotic dynamic be the result of another wrong turn taken by us moms of a certain age and time?

The morning after the St. Paddy's Day party, I went to the farmers' market with the hope that the fresh food might make me feel better. (I hadn't told Page how much the party conversation had revolved around who had gotten in where, though, given the amount of time she was spending online, I was sure she was in the thick of it.) I found baskets of tender, vulnerable greens. Those precious vegetables, cold and wet in the rootstock, find

Oh, these connections from your child's pain
to your pain. There's really nothing like it,
is there, Mom? The travel time is zip, and it
arrives expanded, amplified, yet broken into
tiny fragments like fireworks exploding under
your skin. Your child's pain *is* your pain. You
signed on for the transfer when you gave birth
to her. Unavoidable, right? Or is there another
way to love your child? Could this symbiotic
dynamic be the result of another wrong turn
taken by us moms of a certain age and time?

the courage to push their heads out of the darkness and reach for
the sun. They stopped me in my tracks. I was marinating in the
pain of my child rejected. How was I going to be strong for her?
I needed to find the courage to push my head out of the darkness
of the night before. Conversations from the party repeated in my
sore (hungover) head.

"Billy didn't apply to UCLA," one of the moms had said, just
as I made my entrance.

Liar, I thought. And then from another, "Connie is just distraught. She called me on the way over and told me that she's making an appointment with Blake's college counselor first thing in the morning. She's not going to accept this."

Pretending it didn't matter, or being pissed off at someone—anyone—and making plans for action, were the only topics of the moms' conversation.

"That's such a cute dress" was merely a momentary respite from the misery of motherhood.

I found the dads outside, smoking cigars, drinking dark beers, and talking about the only college situation on their minds: March Madness. I joined 'em. It was worth the next morning's headache to stay out on the patio, watching basketball and *not* talking about our children. And it gave me a pause from the pain to make a plan. A plan to take care of myself.

So, back at the market, double espresso in hand, I admired the shades of green in the vegetables and worked out a recipe. I had to unearth what this—my—hurt was all about. And then I had to find a way to kick it to the curb and prepare myself for what was next. Good Lord! She had applied to ten colleges, and we'd just had the first response!

"Mom, Mom," I called out to her twice before the tightly sprung aluminum screen door bounced and banged off the jamb.

"I'm in here," she answered, "here" being her bedroom. She was getting ready for her high school class reunion. She was on the decorating committee, just back from the hairdresser's and the VFW, where the small-town gala would be held. Strewn about her bed and open hope chest were yearbooks and commencement programs from 1946 to 1949. On her vanity table beside a neglected cup of coffee, the separating milk making a Saturnian ring on the outside circumference, were bowls of mints in shades of pastel yellows, blues, pinks, and greens. Cut squares of netting and short lengths of satin ribbon cluttered the glass top. I was late coming home because I had taken the second bus, the one that carried the jocks, the band members, and the cheerleaders home after practice—and, that late-spring day, tryouts.

"I didn't make it. I didn't make cheerleader for next year."

It was the first time I had given voice to my devastation. In the locker room, I had kept a stiff upper lip while reading the freshly tacked-up list of the chosen. My name wasn't there. I was a cheerleader no more. I was nothing.

"Hook me up," she said as she lit another Winston and slipped her arms into her Playtex Longline bra. We stood there, both of us facing the round mirror of her vanity, she inspecting the pin curl on her right cheek, I gazing at the moist expanse of her back flanked by the two sides of her corset. I'd been "hooking her up" for years. (Brother Scotty and sister Louie were called into service if I wasn't around.) Like the scales on a metal fish, there were three vertical rows of silver loops on the right and one vertical row of hooks on the left.

"Mom!"

"Start at the bottom with the second"—she exhaled a plume of smoke—"but I think we can do the third row for tonight."

"Mom, I didn't make cheerleader!" I repeated while she instinctively sucked in her breath like Scarlett O'Hara as I tugged and stretched the two sides of her essential foundation. Underneath the mess on her vanity top were a few photographs. She picked one up and sighed.

"Nell DellaValle was a cheerleader. She died horribly on Devil's Elbow just two weeks before graduation. I still miss her every day."

"Is that supposed to make me feel better? At least I won't die in a car crash because I'm not a cheerleader anymore!" I finished with the top hooks fastened at the tightest position and worked my practiced way back down to the bottom, inching each miniature claw over until she was all "hooked up" on position svelte. She slid her hands down the front, encircled the cinched-in waist, and turned to face me.

"Toni, I don't think you were much of a cheerleader."

"Yes, I was!" I said with more anger than conviction, because really, my splits were great and my cartwheel was like a starfish, but my front flip was kinda sketchy. Truth was, I knew deep down that my less-than-solid handspring wasn't the shortcoming that got me bumped off the bumpkin squad. I liked the precision of the cheer routines, the royal-blue-and-white pom-poms, and I definitely liked the pleated shirt and saddle shoes. Yes, there was a status, too. But the belonging was the depth of it. Being part of a team made me feel like I was cared for. Sadly for me that day, the judges must have remembered that my love of cheering extended only to the package of being a cheerleader and to my camaraderie with the other girls on the squad. One winter night that previous basketball season, we (the boys) had lost a close game. I had been the only cheerleader not crying. Pretty sure that sealed my fate.

Still, I was angry with my mother for not being the kind of mom (like in the movies!) who stopped everything she was doing to make me a comforting cup of tea, pet my sad brow, and take us to a Broadway show and then dinner at Sardi's. Before she said it, I was mad at her for seeing right through me and into the truth.

"Honey, do you really think you are meant to stand on the sidelines and cheer while the boys run by on their way to glory?" Mom was a Presbyterian. She believed in predestination. "From the first moment I held you in my arms, I knew that you were destined to leave here. To have more than"—she stretched out her hand palm up, floating over the artifacts of her high school years—"this."

She stubbed out her cigarette, took a sip of that hours-old cold coffee, and said, "Here, help me make the favors," as she handed me the prototype bundle of mints, netting, and ribbon. The telephone rang, and I was left alone with a task, the perfect Puritan antidote for self-pity.

I hadn't thought about that day for almost thirty-five years, and why the keen memory of my mother visited me between baskets of frisée and artichokes, I can only imagine. It was a gift bestowed. Mother's love when I needed it the most. Of course, in her fashion, it was an example of what not to do. She did not give energy to my disappointment. God knows she suffered many disappointments in her life, her marriage not the least of them. But when it came to our relationship, she saw a bigger picture. She had been preparing for my exit since the day I was born.

Since that windy March day at the market, I've sent three children off to college, and it does get easier. I won't tell you that their hurts don't affect you—of course they do. You love them. But you don't have to give energy to the things you don't want or things you can't do anything about, which, frankly, girls, is just about everything. Clearly, what you do want is for them to be happy, but you can't make that happen, at least not for very long. I know it is the tritest of self-help clichés, but: All you can really do is make yourself happy, and if you're happy you can spread it around.

That day at the market, I had another flash of memory from the not-too-distant past. Jeff was the coach of the boys' Little League teams. I remembered a teammate from their five-year-old rookie class, long before skill figured into the equation of wearing the uniform. He was on the autism spectrum. We had lost the game, and most of the boys were sad; some were crying. This boy exclaimed to Jeff, as they tossed gloves, bats, and balls into the black canvas duffel bag, "Coach, I'm so glad we won the game!" his smile revealing another day of joy on the ball field.

"No, Timmy, we lost the game. That's why everybody is sad."

"Well, Coach, me being sad isn't gonna make them feel any better."

What do you say to that? I say you adopt that philosophy.

The truth of all of this is that rejection is good. No, seriously, it was especially good for me. It moved me a little step away from the sidelines of my daughter's life and a little closer to the action of mine. Her rejection reminded me once again that I had no control. There was nothing I could do to keep her from experiencing emotional downers. With the gift of a memory of my own rejection, I was granted the grace of perspective. As it turns out, not being part of the squad in my final year of high school opened my mind to the possibility of another identity. An identity that was still in its raw-clay form, but something a little truer to who I really was.

By the time I got home from the market, Page had been accepted at two other colleges: UC Davis and UC Santa Barbara wanted her. She, in her lifelong fashion, was practical about it. She was two for three of the ten colleges she'd applied to. She'd be going to some good school in the fall. I, in my fashion, had visited the depths of despair by expanding her rejection, making it my own by resurrecting my decades-old rejection, yet knowing that this wasn't healthy. That's why it felt so bad. In my life mission to be everything that my mother was not, I hadn't allowed that a good mother could still love fiercely while not making a funeral out of her daughter's disappointment. And the only thing nicer than the feeling of getting over the rejection and feeling better for that experience was experiencing the joy of her acceptances and recognizing that the contrast between the two wasn't that substantial. Because here's the deal, ladies: It's her life. Meanwhile, what's going on with yours?

♡ THE RECIPE

....

La Bagna Cauda (The Hot Bath)

Here's a seasonal, sustainable, and surefire recipe for the college-rejection blues. Find the deepest wound, sit with it, then say goodbye. It works every time.

They said no, she is not invited, and there is nothing you can do about it. The boo-boo is out of the reach of your kisses. You remember the cupcake parties where she didn't make the cut, the prizes she didn't win, the boy who didn't reciprocate her Valentine. Your heart is breaking for her and for you. She will get over this, but you feel obsolete. You can't make it better. You are a mom, and that's what you do. If you can't make it better,

> The pain of saying goodbye is real enough, but it is not about your child. This time, the labor pains you are feeling are for the rebirth of you. It's a long process, and you can do it the hard way or the less-hard way. There is nothing easy about this.

you have no purpose. You, Mom, are worthless. That's what this is really all about.

Indulge yourself in that low energy for as long as you can stand it. Feels like crap, doesn't it? Exhaust that feeling till it shrivels up and dies. And it will, because you know that there is something you *can* do: You can stop that kind of thinking. The pain is real enough, but it is not about your child. This time, the labor pains you are feeling are for the rebirth of you. It's a long process, and you can do it the hard way or the less-hard way. There is nothing easy about this. To help yourself along, you need two baths, one for you and one for the vegetables.

Draw your bath. Doesn't that phrase just evoke comfort? "I'm drawing my bath," you tell a friend who calls to talk (complain, kvetch, fret) to you about her son's college situation. Tell her you'll call her back, but don't. She'll find someone else's ear to fill with her story over and over again. Let her stew in her own juices—you can help only one person at a time, and that person is you. Listen to your flight attendant. When the scary orange oxygen masks fall into your lap, you've gotta put yours on first before you can save anybody else. Light a candle, be extravagant with sea salts, and open up a juicy novel that has nothing to do with kids. Breathe and soak. And let that ball of angst go down the drain with the bathwater. Put on something comfortable, but make sure you feel pretty.

Now make a bath for the vegetables. This simple hot dip transforms beautiful green vegetables into an artistic masterpiece bursting with color and flavor. When I made this dish in my cooking classes, my ladies commented that the *bagna cauda* was great straight off the fingertips. I love that kind of culinary thinking. By March, those girls were coming around.

What You Need

½ cup nice olive oil

2 tablespoons butter

1 tablespoon minced garlic

1–2 tablespoons anchovy paste

Salt

Pepper

Fresh spring vegetables

Instructions

In a little sauté pan, heat olive oil and butter. Squeeze in anchovy paste. Add garlic. Cook until fragrant, but do not let the garlic get brown. Add salt and pepper to taste. Keep warm.

Peel and/or blanch your favorite, freshest vegetables. Nests of frisée, cups of endive, tender inside celery stalks, and early spring greens are perfect raw. I like to blanch asparagus, broccoli, or any vegetable that has too much bite.

Blanching is as easy as boiling water and filling a bowl with ice. Drop the vegetable pieces into boiling, salted water for about 2 minutes. Remove with a slotted spoon or rubber-covered tongs, and immediately submerge them in a large bowl of ice water. This simple process stops the cooking and keeps the vegetables bright and crisp.

Once the temperature of the vegetables decreases, which should take about five minutes, remove with a large slotted spoon or tongs and dry on a tea towel. Arrange on a warm platter around the "hot bath." If you have ramekins that fit in the metal stands that suspend over a tealight, using them is a nice way to keep the bath hot. The best way to serve the *bagna cauda* is in the individual bowls or ramekins; it keeps the dipping and biting noncommunal.

March

She did the work, she stayed in weekends for the extra credit, she took the test four times and raised her score each time. But they don't want her. What are you going to do, Mom?

✓ To Do: *Help Out at a Homeless Shelter*
What does this have to do with your baby's rejection? Everything. You can't help your child navigate life's lessons—they are hers alone, and this is growth for her and for you, too. So what can you do with your valuable and keenly practiced *I want to*

make this better juju? You can help those who are so lost that the starting point for them is not how bummed out they are, but how hungry they are. You can help so many with your mothering love at your local food bank or soup kitchen. And they'll appreciate it more, too.

8 · Acceptances (or, If We Were Salmon, This Would Be the End)

....

APRIL
RECIPE: *Il Timballo*

I regularly run into my cooking-class ladies and other senior-year moms at the post office. Like I said before, they should put a bar in here. It seems that we are at the Post Office more often this senior-year month of April. We are the first to know whether it will be good news or bad news for our seniors. So far on Page's list, only the UCs have notified the applicants online. Acceptances from other schools roll in the old-school way, with color brochures and dormitory forms to fill out. Tugging the fatty packets to extrude them from the narrow mail slot is happy work for Mom. We'll bring them home, lay them out on the kitchen table like the prizes they are, and surprise our senior with yet another possibility. But there are also the sad, thin envelopes that hardly need to be opened.

"Oh, no!" Tabitha said. She held two thin envelopes with similar-looking embossed lettering and crests emblazoned in the left-hand corners—the only apparent difference being the colors of the crests and the names of the schools underneath.

"Bob isn't going to like this. We knew Yale was a stretch," she said, separating the two envelopes, holding one in each hand, "but Brown? It's Bob's alma mater."

"I thought you said last week that Will is really excited about Colorado."

"Yeah, Will is. We're not." She separated the rest of the mail and slid the two unopened envelopes into her turquoise Kate Spade bag. "I better make that sweet-potato gnocchi for dinner tonight. Bob is going to be so pissed off at the admissions department. Especially after all he's done for them."

I don't know how Tabitha does it. She just keeps chugging along, doing everything for everybody. And she looks great and happy doing it! She opens up her home for every worthy cause, my cooking classes included, volunteers at church and three schools, manages her large extended families, and has raised the nicest kids.

The week before, I had seen Will at Cafe Marmalade, reading the newspaper. Reading the newspaper! As always, he said hello, asked about Page (they were together from kindergarten through the eighth grade, before he attended a private high school in San Francisco), and was quick to offer enthusiastic responses to my typical mom questions.

"How's it going with the college scene, Will? Have you heard from any schools?" I asked him while I waited for my latte.

"Not the ones from the East yet, but I got in to Colorado," he said, smiling. "I'm so psyched! I love it there! How about Page?"

"She's deciding between Davis, Santa Barbara, American University in Washington, D.C., Tulane, and Vanderbilt in Tennessee, of all places," I said. I was as familiar with her list as I was with the year-round availability of fresh herbs—parsley, sage, rosemary, and thyme—in my garden. Being practical when she had made her list the previous fall, she had included her ultimate safety schools, a couple of state schools. They weren't in the running. She had one school left to hear from—like oregano, the last herb, a standout and not an everyday one, that was for sure.

"Wow, that's a lot of schools. Tell her I said congratulations."

It was a lot of schools, good schools, some with incredible academic-scholarship offers. But something was missing. Page was relieved that she had choices, though I never saw the look in her eyes that Will had when he told me about Colorado. She probably would not choose Davis, as it was only an hour-and-forty-minute drive away. The halfway point on our family ski trips to Tahoe, the place where we stopped for burgers at In-N-Out on the way home, it was too familiar. I liked the idea of driving up for lunch and a girls' day out, but I knew it was too close to home for her. In addition, many of her high school posse were probably going there.

"It's like Redwood High School 2.0," she told me when I started waxing on about how great UC Davis would be for her. For me.

Santa Barbara, six hours away, was perched on a sandy outcropping overlooking the Pacific Ocean, a picturesque California beach scene. UCSB—*U Could Study But* . . . a joke among the very smart kids who got in, though the party reputation was warranted. A SoCal party school and Page? She hadn't applied to the excellent "local" school, UC Berkeley, because it was, well, local. And I got that. I supported that college life should stretch the imagination and experience, and that a change in geography is an experience not to be forgotten, especially if your geography has been the moderate climate of Northern California and the "diversity" of living in Marin County.

When Page was in the process of creating her list of "safety" to "reach" schools, she visited her school's counselor. Mrs. Collins gave her the names and materials of diverse schools in diverse locations from Chicago to New Orleans to Nashville. These schools were great, and far away and different and unknown, physically unknown. We figured that once she got accepted to the school, we'd visit to see if she liked the feel of the place, because I just couldn't afford to take her all over the country on a college tour. So that was the plan. In the meantime, there were websites for the three schools on her list she hadn't seen. That would have to do.

She'd been to the other campuses on her list. The summer before senior year, we took a family road trip down the coast to check out the California public universities, the UCs.

"Page, you can't go here," Ross said as the five of us walked the campus of UCSB. "This isn't your style. Plus, you're too smart to go here. I *know* people who go here."

"Are you kidding? This place is sick, Page." Banks was looking at the strip of sand below the campus. "There's a path to the beach!"

We all weighed in on how the place looked. Maybe not the usual criterion one uses as a valuation of a university. The romantics among us (me) were looking for some stone and ivy. University of Pittsburgh (hail to Pitt!), my alma mater, might not be known for her beauty, but there are some spots there that could be Hogwarts.

When Page was in eighth grade, all her friends were applying to private high schools. I could tell she felt left out; the local public high school was the only option for us. Even though I knew she would thrive there because that larger school would provide her with the freedom to start fresh, like any teenager wants to do, I knew that the choices of the pretty private schools were something she would have enjoyed. Redwood High School would be a place to stretch and bust out of the box that one gets drawn in when attending kindergarten through eighth grade with the same forty-two kids.

"Hillary is applying to five high schools," she told me about her best friend one day in the spring of her eighth-grade and last year at our little town school. "I wonder if I'd get in to Branson." She kind of trailed off as she looked away from me and out the passenger window of the Trooper.

"Honey, do you really want to go to a high school for four years with a class that's not even twice the size of your eighth grade?" I knew she didn't, but I also knew it was something else. She had been striving since first grade. Acceptances to the competitive private high schools would be an important external validation of an identity. Smart Girl. An identity she wanted and had worked hard to create. I remembered her determination to get into the top reading group of Ms. Q's second grade.

"I'm going to try out for the Salamanders," she told me, her s-words making a particularly darling sound coming through the toothless gap where her front baby teeth used to be. In an effort to make the kids feel like they were all the same, that no one was smarter than the next guy, animal names were assigned to the reading groups that separated the "you're going to Harvard" from the "oh, dear, you're struggling" second-grade readers. Page was a Newt, the middle amphibian. But you know the kids know what's what. And they are fine with it. Of course the moms were worried that their seven-year-old would feel badly if a distinction was made, that damage would be done to their psyche if differences were acknowledged, and the moms were a force. So there was this artificial setup. Unlike at my elementary school, there was no A reading group, B reading group, and Holy Shit, Good Thing You Still Have the Farm reading group. They moved the reading amphibians around to different tables, and they read at changing times of the morning, Tuesdays and Thursdays one week, Mondays and Wednesdays the next. But like I said, the kids knew. My message to Page was: *If you are a Newt, that's just fine. I love Newts, but this is America, and if you want to be a Salamander, you can work for it.*

It took her three tries. Once my little Newt became a Salamander, there was no stopping her. Ultimately, she accepted that she probably could have gotten in to the competitive private high schools. I offered to pay for the application fees, we could go through the process like her friends, but she knew that we couldn't afford the tuition. Page, being Page, accepted the logic that it was a moot point. There would be money for college. And I wanted her to get into a pretty college unlike the public high school she would attend, albeit a strong academic one, but one that had been designed by the same firm that erected prisons in 1960s California.

So, here we were, ten years after her transformation into a Salamander, and four years past her acceptance that external academic recognition would have to wait. We were getting close to picking one of the many fine universities that had offered her an acceptance.

It was Easter Sunday evening. The five of us had joined Jeff's parents for a decadent lunch buffet at the Palace Hotel in downtown San Francisco. The clothes that had fit earlier that morning had felt like they belonged to someone else (a smaller someone else) on the ride home to Marin. When we got home, panty hose and neckties were peeled off faster than the shells of the jumbo shrimp we had consumed. Jeff and I were sprawled on the couches in the living room, wearing things with elastic waists. I don't remember what the boys were doing. I was in a sushi, brioche, filet mignon, crépe suzette coma. And then we heard what sounded like a squeal coming from Page's room. The girl whom I had been trying to rev up all our lives together was beside herself, outside herself, with vocal demonstrations of excitement. "Glee" is the word I would use. Northwestern. She had clicked on the screen of her pink iMac and found that she had been accepted to Northwestern, her "reachiest" of reach schools, the highest-ranked one on her list, the brightest star shining on the shores of Lake Michigan.

As promised, we booked a flight to Chicago and attended the "prospy" (prospective student) weekend. It was organized like a state dinner. The parents were treated like foreign dignitaries with name badges, seminars, and linen-tablecloth lunches. The prospective students were treated like the academic stars they were. Generous current Northwestern freshmen invited the high school seniors to spend one of the two nights we were there at their dorm. I met some of the kids, her fellow prospies. They were cheerful and polite, and most were still deciding between a handful of schools. I was just beaming. I was so happy for my daughter.

"Mommy, this is a safety school for most of these kids," Page told me after spending the night in Hinman Hall, the dorm that would ultimately be her home for the upcoming academic year. "Most of the kids I talked to are deciding between Princeton, Yale, and here, unless they get into MIT or Harvard, so it's not that big a deal."

"Oh, sure it's not! It's not a big deal at all," I teased her over our first deep-dish Chicago-style pizza.

Acceptance hadn't changed her. She wasn't full of herself,

and by nature landed on understatement, but I knew she was impressed and I knew that she would pick Northwestern. Who cared if they had only one class she was interested in? Taking in the stone, brick, and ivy, not to mention the private Lake Michigan beachfront, sealed the deal. There was no point in visiting Tulane or Vanderbilt. Neither Santa Barbara nor Davis could hold a candle to the light of Northwestern. This was it. And I couldn't ignore the fact that my darling daughter would be a long plane ride away from me in a few short months.

Back in California, I prepared for my Girls' Night Out cooking class. Usually the classes were luncheon ones, sandwiched between the drop-off and pickup of our kids. Earlier in the spring, Priscilla, the director of our town recreation department, had suggested we offer an evening one.

"There's not that much going on in April," she said. "And this could be a way for you to expand *la cucina semplice*." She pronounced it *la koo-seen-a sam-place*.

What a lovely lady Priscilla is! She's always looking out for me, offering encouragement. But good God, if only she, after ten months of hearing me say it, could pronounce the name of my cooking-class business. It's not her fault. Nobody can. The Simple Kitchen, La Cucina Semplice, was a succinct description of exactly what I had to offer. I thought it was a brilliant name. And I was sorta getting into the branding of me, and I thought that if I just kept saying it enough, La Cucina Semplice would become a household name.

Unfortunately, though "the simple kitchen" is easy to say in English, and *la cucina semplice* is easy to say in Italian (if you speak Italian), *la cucina semplice* is a real bear for native English speakers. *La* is *la*, okay. *Koo-cheen-aah*, doable. But *sehm-plea-chay*, accent on the first syllable, never comes out right. For those of you, dear readers, who may be inspired by the idea of launching an enterprise dear to your heart after the kids leave, here's some free, slowly learned wisdom. First rule of making a new business: Don't name it something that is difficult to say. Follow-up rule: Don't spend all your start-up money—in my case, $600—on a logo and stickers with the difficult name. But the logo was adorable and the custard-and-caramel-colored stickers were bee-you-ti-full! So I planned to make this work. If Volkswagen could get Americans to say *fahrvergnügen*, how hard could it be?

I think I want that on my tombstone. "How hard could it be?" pretty much sums up my misplaced outlook on just about every-thing. So, how hard is it going to be moving into the next part of my life? Ha! How hard is it going to be to throw myself into my fledging but promising cooking-class business, La Cucina Semplice, while I'm trying to get my footing in this semidepress-ing milestone year of my life? Double ha!

Anyway, linguistics aside, I wasn't the only senior-year mom who needed a night out that April. As soon as the spring bro-chure poked out of the post office boxes, two gals bought the whole class for a birthday party. I added another one, and that one sold out, too. I decided to teach my ladies how to make poached salmon with a creamy tomato reduction to spoon over soft rosemary-infused polenta. I used to make this dish every salmon season when the kids were little and, being little (and especially the boys being boys), they were suspicious of "fish."

"Mommy, what's for dinner?" Ross or Banks would ask pretty much every evening after an afternoon of play. A couple of Fred

Flintstones, those two were clear about the time of day and their expected dinner, and that there should be some woman fixing it.

"Chicken."

"It doesn't smell like chicken."

"It's the pink chicken," I'd tell them. I held the same confidence that they'd believe me as when I had told them that a large bunny was going to come into the house at night while we slept and drop off baskets full of chocolates.

"Do we like the pink chicken?"

"You love pink chicken!" Actually, they did and do. Could have been the pungent tomato sauce or my brainwashing, but I gotta give it up to the shiny, fresh, gorgeous salmon.

Pacific salmon are incredible, both in taste and in lifestyle, if you can call it that. When it's time to spawn, they find their way back from their high-seas adventures to the little stream where they were born by way of a mysterious mechanism. Those poor pink mommy fishes struggle upstream just to get "home" so they can carry on their fishy family line, send their kids off to college, and die. I tell this to my Girls' Night Out students as I show them how to remove the thin white bones from the solid coral flesh. Several of my lunchtime ladies are enjoying cosmopolitans; they aren't much help with the boning. The class has that naughty "out on a school night" feeling. We drink, eat, and laugh. Just days back from Chicago, I can't take my mind off the determined salmon. Hopefully, Page has that mechanism to find her way home again.

April is the month of acceptance. That sounds good. This should be a cheery chapter! Acceptance conjures up this wonderful feeling of being included, invited to the party, the opposite of

April is the month of acceptance. All the

hard work has paid off, and they want you.

Acceptance letters will rain down on you

and your senior like so many April showers.

Fat packages full of freshman information

will arrive in your mailbox and pile up on

your senior's desk. What else does the word

acceptance conjure for you? Sometimes

acceptance means suck it up, get over it, and

keep your unhappiness to yourself.

rejected. You got in! All the hard work has paid off, and they want you. Acceptance letters will rain down on you and your senior like so many April showers. Fat packages full of freshman information will arrive in your mailbox and pile up on your senior's desk. You did include the "sure thing" safety colleges on your list last fall, right? Of course, you did, Smart Mom.

Maybe a "stretch" school has offered your daughter a spot. Happy, Happy, Joy, Joy! All things—including financial considerations—being equal between the colleges that have accepted your senior, each one would be a great choice. It's just a matter of personal taste. Maybe you are deciding between the solid final two—you know, like *American Idol*. But unlike the democratic voting process that you enjoy from the couch (texting in your choice between the cute country-singer girl and the cute rocker guy), in this case, your vote doesn't count. It's her call. Period. Accept that, Mom.

What? That kind of acceptance is just a big fat downer. That kind of acceptance sounds like swallowing a bitter pill. All your life, well-meaning folks (people you are probably sick of) have been telling you "you just have to accept it"—"it" being anything you don't want in your life. Acceptance means suck it up, get over it, and keep your unhappiness to yourself. But pretty soon you're getting fat from eating your words and accepting a pile of rubbish you don't want. You just keep taking it in and storing it away. Why do you do that?

A mom is walking through a gravel field.

"There's a pebble in my shoe," she says. "I'm going to stop walking for a second and take it out."

"Nope," says the gravel field, "you're just going to get more pebbles in your shoes—might as well get used to it."

The mom accepts the logic and the uncomfortable (but not unbearable) pebble and keeps trudging. Her husband has to cross the gravel field, too. He gets a pebble in his shoe. He stops, swears, and throws the pebble thirty yards. This happens many times. He's in the moment. He's furious. He calls his pal with the bulldozer and clears a path. But there's another gravel field in the distance. And another one after that. The gravel fields stretch endlessly. He'll deal with that when he gets there. He's got a bulldozer.

Acceptance or resistance? Deal with it or fix it? They might appear to be polar opposites, but at the core they are the same thing. Either way, there is no choice in the story. Accepting is a passive verb, an internal reaction to something unwanted. Resisting might seem like an action verb because it takes so much outward energy. But you're just fighting, fighting, fighting in visible, external reaction to something you don't want. Same thing. Neither one of these approaches is sustainable.

She'd get another wacky idea; they were weekly, these ideas of hers. She was full of energy even though she was a full-time housewife and mother. She'd delicately sprinkle it, the idea, into the breakfast conversation she shared with her husband. He'd rattle the newspaper and say, "No!" like a father to his daughter. After she kissed him goodbye at the threshold, he'd go off to work and she'd forget all about the "No!" and start laying the groundwork for her idea. Things would go sideways, he'd find out, and boy, he'd be pissed off. When he found out what she'd been up to—making salad dressing to sell, or auditioning for a small part in a show—which was inevitable, as his discovery was part of the seed planted in the fertile ground of the idea, he'd yell and swear, usually in that foreign language of his. And then he'd raise his hand to her. She'd cower and put her hands up to protect herself from the blows that were threatened but never came, because this was a television show and it was just Ricky being mad at Lucy. There was no public outrage that a husband would smack his wife if she got out of line, defied him. It was just accepted. More than accepted, it

was funny. Like the bus-driving Ralph—"Why, I oughta . . . "—
before him, Ricky was just a guy being a guy with a wife. Truth
was, some folks thought a slap would be for Lucy's own good.
As the episode came to its happy conclusion, she'd say she was
sorry and they'd head off to the club and dance. *Da da daaa, da
da daaa, da da.*

"That's just the way that generation was," Scotty said with a
shrug. "It was the culture, and a lot of men were like that."

This stupid argument—that if a lot of people are doing "it,"
whatever "it" is—has been used to tolerate and accept extraor-
dinarily unacceptable behavior. The position that it is a cultural
dynamic adds enough fog to the bullshit, affording one the luxury to look the other way, to not exactly see it, or to remember
it as "not that bad," which legitimizes the abuser—"Well, she
shoulda listened to him"—and puts the victim in a position of
accountability.

Usually it would start softly. They'd be in the bedroom talking,
and Dad would be getting dressed to go to work. Something
would irritate him, just set him off. It could be the way she'd
ironed or hadn't ironed the crease in his slacks, a spot on the
wall-to-wall carpeting, a button missing on her blouse. Then—
smash—you'd hear the coffee cup shatter against the wall, his
booming, baritone, God-like voice: "How many times do I have
to tell you . . ." a slap, a cry, a slammed door, his exit. And then—
and this is the best part—she'd come out humming. Scotty and I
would be huddled in our room or in the kitchen, eating *spranglin
calabro*, just back from the paper route, and Mom would come
out from the scene in their bedroom, looking for a tea towel to
soak up the coffee, her cheek painted with a tattoo of rising red
welts from his fingers, humming. Like we didn't know what had

happened. If pretending was a magical spell that could change the past, my mom was Merlin.

I first heard this story in church; it was part of the sermon. One of those folksy parables told to express a larger point about how we end up in a place in our lives or in our relationships that we never would have agreed to if the current state were presented to us at the git-go. Well known as the "How do you cook a frog?" speech, it stuck with me. And when I have found myself in a shitty mess—a.k.a. hot water—with my husband, kids, or friends, I think of that frog in the cool water, welcoming the slight warmth that the flame underneath the pot is producing. You know the trajectory of Froggie's plight, right? If he had landed in that boiling water, he would have jumped right out, but when the temperature goes from cool to warm to "oh, really warm!" you just keep swimming around. Until your muscles are too cooked to move, and then you're done.

What the Pastor wanted us to understand was that unbearable conditions in our lives didn't start out that way. Of course they didn't, because if on your first date the guy yelled at you for laughing too loudly, you'd say, "Goodbye, creep." So how do we go from the honeymoon to living with abuse? Just a little acceptance at a time.

How's the water, Froggie?

Morally we can see that the abuser is clearly the bad guy. There's no platform for him to stand on and make it okay. It's all his fault. He's dishing it out, and she's just gotta take it. That's the relationship. But aren't there two of them in this relationship? Is the acceptor blameless? There is nothing she can do, right? Nope, not if you believe in the story of the victim. You have to believe that the power is outside you to buy into the victim mentality. You have to believe that power can be taken away from you for this model to work. And you have to accept that the role you are playing in this drama is not your choice.

After I had been away at college for a semester, it was as if, unbeknownst to me, I was becoming a new frog, a mutation away from the role that the years of complicit acceptance demanded of me as a member of our family. My newly formed tadpole was not accepting of the boiling water of my dad's anger toward my mom. And I recognized something that was there all along. The powder keg of his anger was exclusively for her. My childhood was not scarred with beatings he gave out to us kids. Quite the contrary: He was the dad who flew kites with us, extended bedtimes, played ball, taught me how to ride a bike, taught me how to dance, taught me how to swear. No, the verbal and physical abuse was something caught up in the intimacy of their relationship.

One weekend during a visit home from college, we were in the kitchen, talking about the upcoming election, when my mom reached over my dad's lap to pour him more coffee. He started in on how stupid she was.

"Debby, how many times do I have to tell you that you could spill the hot coffee on my legs?" His volume increasing. And you know what? She had burned him, she had burned him several times. Once with hot oil as she slid his eggs from the frying pan onto his plate and drizzled the oil onto the hem of his Bermuda shorts, down the exposed skin of his thighs, onto his tender white feet. He started in on his all-too-familiar amped-up path to righteous rage. She backed away in expectant fear.

"I'm sorry, Rudy," she said. She delivered her worn-out lines like a leading actress deigning to take a supporting part in a production that was beneath her abilities and stature.

I was considered a pretty tough nut in our family. As the oldest of four, I was the leader of our childhood pack of my brother, Scotty, his friends, and our male cousins. The tears that streamed down my face stopped the momentum of their played-out drama.

"I can't stand this. Stop it," I said. I don't think it was my words that froze their scene that morning. I think it was the freedom that emanated from me. I wasn't in this anymore. I wasn't responsible for the unfair hurts my mom endured. I wasn't responsible for the troubles my dad had to shoulder. I would no longer accept that "this was just the way things were" and play my small but important role as witness to their tragedy.

But I didn't move to resistance, either. I wasn't about to fix this. I had lived my young life bouncing between acceptance and resistance. There were years in high school when I championed her cause and tried to get my mom to fight back.

"He's such an ass. There's a name for what he is. It's 'wife-beater.' You could call the sheriff. You could kick him out."

"He's your father. I never want to hear you say those things again."

I wasn't alone in trying to help my mom. My dad's sisters didn't think his behavior was right, but they were perplexed about why my mom continued to do the things she did, or *not* do the things that were expected of her. It was always the same dumb housekeeping deficits that set him off. That and the way she looked most days, wearing soiled, tattered clothes when nice ones were in her closet. She seemed over her head with housework, and there were more days than not when I'd come home from school to find beds unmade, dishes in the sink, no dinner started, and the feathered imprint of the chenille bedspread on her face betraying an afternoon spent reading, sleeping, and smoking. She'd look at the clock, jump to action like the house was on fire, and tell me to get to work. "We'd better vacuum the living room before your father gets home," she'd say. "We," which meant me.

"Debby, I'll help you with the laundry. You've got to get those curtains back up before Rudy gets home," Aunt Sue said. Of all my aunts, my mom was closest to her, and though Mom's treatment at Dad's hands was no secret, I think there were occasions when Mom dropped the humming denial ("What happened to your eye, Debby?" "You know how clumsy I am—I walked into the door") and confided in Aunt Sue about the more authentic, deeper pain.

I was closest to Aunt Sue, too. It was the biggest compliment to me when my dad or other aunties would say, "Toni, you're just like Sue," as I was espousing my strong positions on topics that ranged from politics to the character of the characters starring in the afternoon soaps. Aunt Sue smiled and laughed easily, but her eyes held the history of the life she had lived as someone whose childhood had ended abruptly. My grandmother died in childbirth, and Aunt Sue, being the oldest girl, had to quit school and care for her younger siblings and older brothers. She did not have an easy life, but she moved through it with grace. Sometimes, after a particularly bad time with my dad, my mom would walk across the field to Aunt Sue's house for a cup of coffee. After those visits, I could see the suffering it caused Aunt Sue to be privy to the disturbing details of the relationship between her little brother and her best friend.

"Fix yourself up, honey. Put on some lipstick." (This from

Aunt Josefina.) "You'll feel better if you look better." Aunt Josefina lived by this motto. And she was right. You *do* feel better
if you look better. As long as I can remember, I was part of the
circle of these women, these housewives. I think I was accepted
as "one of them" since I did more of the housewifery than my
mom did. As my young self started to form the idea of what a
woman was supposed to be, I looked to my Italian aunties. Not
to my mom. She was a disaster. Keep the house clean, make a
nice dinner, freshen up and dress pretty before your husband
comes home. It seemed so simple. Look, they were all doing it,
and their husbands, my uncles, were nice to them. But Mom
stubbornly resisted their suggestions. It was as if she purposely
wanted to irritate my dad. Or it seemed that way to me. I don't
know. I was a kid. How can anyone ever know what is inside
someone else's marriage?

"I loved your mother dearly," Aunt Carmella told me when
we talked after my mom's funeral, "but she never should have
married your father. She was not equipped to handle an Italian
husband or a household. She wasn't a housewife, your mom."

No, she wasn't, and that's not a crime. Spousal abuse is. Pulling your kids into your unhealthy relationship, making them
complicit in the pretending, accepting that they just have to bear
witness, should be. As the oldest, and a girl, I probably soaked up
the worst of the conflicting emotions, but as the oldest, I know
I also got the best of them. And the gift—and I believe there is
always a gift, if we choose to open it—is that the responsibili-
ties that were dished out to me at a very early age gave me the
confidence to leave my parents, which gave me the space to see
them. To see my parents as people.

I was over playing my part in the soap opera of our family as either one of the helpless characters of Acceptance or

Resistance. Did my epiphany come from God? I don't know, but I had landed on the divine gift of allowing. You think there's no distinction between acceptance and allowing, just a little word play? Try this: Say, "I accept," and say, "I allow," and tell me you don't feel the difference. I don't know if it was the small distance college had afforded me, but the clarity on the day I finally put my foot down was undeniable. The tears that rolled down my cheeks weren't accompanied by sobs. It was a release. I let go. And in that moment, I made a choice to allow my parents to be whatever they wanted to be. I felt filled with light. I experienced the first taste of my own true power. Choosing to allow.

Before I was a restaurant owner and a mom, I worked in cancer research. One of my duties was enrolling patients in experimental therapy, the kind of frontline stuff that raises hopes and raises the stock market value of the pharmaceutical company. To qualify for these treatments, the patient had to have already exhausted the traditional therapies. By the time they got to me, they were pretty beat up. Desperate to "keep fighting," they traveled across the country for this last chance. I'd take their medical history to determine if they fit the protocol, and in hearing their life history, I got to know them. They had wives and children and brothers and mothers who loved them. But here they were, in their greatest hour of stress, in San Francisco, apart from their loved ones. Because . . .

Because we are trained to ignore the biggest, most inevitable fact of our existence: the fact that this will ultimately come to an end. For our parents, us, our kids, their kids. Everybody dies. Where we go is the mystery. But in the meantime, what we have here is the real miracle.

Go back to Iowa and smell the fresh-cut grass of the golf course you love. Go back to Brooklyn and eat that greasy hot dog that you have denied yourself in the name of health. Stop spending your final days fighting in hospitals. Get back to the loving. You have a choice. Those were the things I wanted to say, but it wasn't my place.

I noticed an interesting phenomenon when, because of one lab result or another, the patient did not qualify for the experimental treatment. Relief. The pure feeling of relief when a painful choice is taken away. Another paradox. We think that our freedom hinges on our ability to make a choice, yet removing the choice from the equation often meant a huge burden was lifted from their shoulders. The deeper truth is that what they were doing—accepting the misery of one hammer-like treatment after another and resisting the disease—wasn't really a choice. Now, they no longer had to resist and accept. They could just allow life to be what it was: a finite number of days, but an infinite quantity of love. All that was left was to go home. It was as if they needed permission to stop battling.

I read similar phrases of valiant conflict coming from the frontlines of the war on death in the daily obituaries. I like the obituaries. (Shut up! I'm a Scorpio.) *After a hard-fought battle with lung cancer . . . After a two-year fight . . . She never gave up fighting . . .* I imagine you know who won. Yeah, that would be the Grim Reaper. He always wins. So why would you want to play when the deck is stacked? Screw him! Start a new game with rules that can change with your mood, a game you always win because the only object of the game is love.

The choice is yours. Really. Okay, so life is a smorgasbord, a buffet. We can choose the things we want and pass on the things we don't want. But for some reason we tend to focus on the unwanted things. If Sally chooses the wrong school—i.e., the one you don't want her to attend—that's all you're going to

Whether it's your first child or your last to step
into the next phase of her life, it's time for you
to exercise the control you have over *your* life.
Consider that you can imagine bad things and
good things. Own the fact that you can choose
which story you want to tell yourself. Choose
the one that feels better. It's as simple as that.

think about. Choose to change that. Her choice is the first of
many she will make as she sets out to claim her life. And your
choice, Mom, is to be happy for her or to be worried for her.
Come on! You want me to tell you the second option is not
available to you? Okay, you have to be happy.

Yes, I know this is good advice, and easier said than done,
right? On the surface, that's true. You can't talk yourself into
happiness if your emotions are having their way with you, boiling under your skin. But try taking a breath. Recognize that you
are thinking your way down the path of unhappiness. You say,
"This is how I feel, and there's nothing I can do about that."
Then you can support your shitty-feeling position with state-
ments like "I just don't see him there. I know him. That school
is too big. He'll get lost. That school is too small. He'll be bored.

He needs structure. He needs an open curriculum." And the list of how you know what is best for another human being goes on. I challenge you to ask yourself, "Why do I think that?" Demand a full accounting of why you are in your right to feel so poorly. I bet there are some holes in that argument.

Mom, it's April of senior year. Whether it's your first child or your last to step into the next phase of her life, it's time for you to exercise the control you have over *your* life. Consider that you can imagine bad things and good things. Own the fact that you can choose which story you want to tell yourself. Choose the one that feels better. It's as simple as that.

This month's recipe will give you a great opportunity to choose, but you've got to put it all in the mix. There's a creamy risotto crust holding in all the secrets of the kitchen. Pearls of mozzarella, baby peas bathed in a prosciutto-infused tomato *ragù*, chicken livers, and mushrooms. You can adore the zucchini *dore*, and he can wolf down the meatballs. The dish has something for everyone, and maybe some things you don't like. You might be surprised that your palate has changed. Give it a try. Like the richness and contrast of life, choice is there for you in the buffet of the *timballo*.

The first time I made the *timballo*, I was planning on teaching it the next day.

"This is certainly straying from your 'simple kitchen,'" Page pointed out to me as I layered strips of zucchini *dore* over a *ragù* of peas and prosciutto.

"Well, the prep is, I guess, but the simple part is that after it's in the oven, all you need is a simple butter-lettuce salad as a starter, and the whole impressive dinner is held together in one beautiful arborio hatbox," I said as I packed the remaining rice onto the top of the shell over the goodies. "*Molto semplice*," I affirmed as I slid my heavy creation into the warm oven.

"Have you ever made this before?"

"No. But I've seen it before." Though the last time had probably been forty years ago.

"And you're going to teach this tomorrow?" she asked me, with the tone in her voice that I've come to recognize as her polite way of saying, *You are crazy.*

The timballo was a delicious hit, and it came out of the mold sorta-kinda okay. I ruminated about how I could improve the rice crust.

"How can you attempt to teach something that you've made only once, with less-than-perfect results?" Page asked me after we'd all had second helpings.

"I don't know, honey, I guess I think things have a way of working out," I said to her on the Tuesday night before Easter Sunday.

♡ THE RECIPE

* *

Il Timballo

This *timballo* was the rarest of dishes from my childhood memories. It was prepared by the oldest Italian ladies in town and was saved for christenings or the welcoming of a new priest. It was a group effort assembled in the church kitchen with the specialties of each of the *strega nonnas* layered on top of one another like the stories of their lives. It was presented with the ceremony of a wedding cake, the first cut made by the priest.

My memory of the *timballo* and Mrs. Rossi, who every winter scolded Scotty and me for sledding on her hill but at the end of the day always had a hot *cioccolata* waiting for us, is the inspiration for this recipe.

The pan, which had the lore of being the only vessel outside of Italy that could bake the *timballo*, was essentially a flat-topped, round, ceramic cake pan that measured about fourteen inches in diameter, six inches high. If you can source one from a restaurant-supply store, great, but if you can find an aluminum wedding-cake pan, that works just fine, too. I wouldn't try to make the *timballo* in a disposable aluminum roasting pan, because you need to push the rice into the sides and the roasting pan is too thin to stand up to the volume and the heat.

What You Need

3 cups arborio rice

⅓ cup butter for the rice and more for the pan

1 cup parmigiana

3 whole eggs

Your imagination, to make the layers of filling

Instructions

Okay, this strays from the *semplice*, but once it's in the oven, your work is done, except for a bit of praying you need to do to ensure that it comes out of the pan in one piece.

Butter your pan really generously and thoroughly. The butter helps the *timballo* slide out, and it also adds flavor to the crust. You can dust your buttered pan with either seasoned or plain breadcrumbs. What goes into the rice box can run from seafood to sausage to vegetable to cheese to any combination thereof. Traditionally, chicken livers and meatballs show up in many *timballi*, but the filling can be anything. A simple sausage sauce, some sautéed vegetables, and *boccocini* (little pearls of fresh mozzarella) make a great filling.

To make the rice, set to boiling a large quantity of salted water. Like, 2 gallons in a stockpot. Add arborio rice. Once you've got the water rumbling, the rice will tumble and dance. (By the way, if you remember October's recipe, this is nothing like the process of making risotto. Same grain, different application.)

After the rice bubbles for 15 minutes, drain it and place it in a bowl that holds 1/3 cup butter cut into about five pieces. The heat from the rice will melt the butter. Mix it gently, and then spread the rice out on a baking sheet to cool.

Mix parmigiana and eggs (whipped till the whites and yolks are smooth) into the slightly cooled rice. When you take some of the mixture in your hand and squeeze it, it should hold the shape of your hand. Spread about three-quarters of it on the bottom and work it up the sides in equal depth to make a "rice box."

What do you want to fill your *timballo* with? I like to layer long rectangles of vegetables over crumbly sausage and dot a *ragù* with tiny balls of mozzarella. Zucchini *dore* is worth the effort to add to the mix. Depending on the season, the dark-green skin of the zucchini can be bitter. You might want to peel most of it away. I like to cut the zucchini lengthwise after discarding the first cut of skin. (You can also make "coins.") *Dore* is a simple process involving flour, egg, oil, salt, and pepper. You can season the flour with salt and pepper or even a pinch of dried herbs.

Dredge the cut zucchini slices in the flour; shake off any flour

that is not clinging to the vegetable. The juice from the cut zucchini should be enough moisture to hold the flour.

Whip up 2 whole eggs until the white and yolk are blended.
Dip the flour-covered strips or coins of zucchini in the egg and
immediately lay them down in the hot oil of your fry pan. The
egg should puff out of the edges but not turn brown. You don't
need to cook the zucchini completely, as they will be in the oven
for 40 minutes, so just turn them over after about 30 seconds,
fry the other side, and remove with a fork to a plate covered with
a paper towel. Okay, there's one simple step done.

Sauté some bulk sausage (the loose kind, not the kind in cas-
ings) till crumbly and set aside. Better yet (or in addition, if
you're inclined to the carnivorous like I am), make some tiny
meatballs like we made in the *pallottoline in brodo* (January's
soup class). My meatballs generally include grass-fed beef, oats,
fresh parsley (lots of it, so the bright green shows through),
garlic, parmigiana, egg, Italian dried-herb mix (oregano, sage,
thyme), and salt and pepper to taste. If you make tiny meatballs,
you can put them into the *timballo* raw. Line them up on a piece
of wax paper and allow them to come to room temperature.

I want to talk about temperature of food here and the American panic over raw beef, rare ground beef, pink juicy pork, and
the resultant cooking practices that have come from a place of
fear. I have witnessed many of my friends toss an icebox-cold
piece of chicken or beef directly into a pan. They claim they
are using one of my recipes. In Dorie Greenspan's immaculate
cookbook *Around My French Table*, she relates a story of being
observed washing the chicken she was preparing to make for
dinner by none other than her friend and all-star chef Jacques
Pépin. He asks her what the hell she is doing. When she explains,

he shrugs (I imagine) as only a Frenchman can and says that where he comes from, the chickens do not need to be washed.

I suggest you buy this amazing cookbook not only for the recipes and tantalizing food-porn photos, but because Dorie, in addition to being a James Beard Award winner, is a terrific story-teller and first-class writer. My point is that even the esteemed Ms. Greenspan fell prey to the American food-safety fears that swirl up like little tornadoes every couple of months.

I belong to Slow Food, an international organization that Carlo Petrini founded in Italy. In general response to the unsafe and wasteful policies of food globalization, and specifically to protest a proposal for a McDonald's to be built at the foot of the Spanish Steps in Rome, Petrini started the movement. From the website: "Slow Food is an idea, a way of living and a way of eating. It is part of a global, grassroots movement with thousands of members in over 150 countries, which links the pleasure of food with a commitment to community and the environment."

Many amazing people are writing about, talking about, and working toward a better food supply for all of us, and if there is one thing you can do, it is this: Know where your food comes from. The closer to home, the better. Okay, I'm off my free-range soapbox now. Thanks for listening.

So, you have the buttered rice cooling, the zucchini *dore* resting on paper towels, the meatballs relaxing (coming up to room temperature) on waxed paper, and the sautéed sausage in a bowl. If you are inclined, make a sauté of chicken livers and crimini mushrooms. They make an earthy addition to the mix. You should also have on hand some small balls of fresh moz-zarella, sometimes called *perlini*, which you can find at most grocery stores. Drain the water, soak up the extra moisture on a couple of paper towels, then toss with a little olive oil, salt, and pepper.

The *ragù* is the last thing you need to do. This simple version adds color and moisture. Sauté some chopped pancetta or prosciutto in 2 teaspoons of oil. (There is enough fat in the pancetta to dry-fry it, but a little olive oil never hurts.) Add some finely chopped shallots, salt, pepper, and a pinch of dried and powdered sage. Add about a cup and a half of frozen petite green peas. The water from the peas will spritz and steam in the pan. That's okay.

Once the peas lose their hard, frozen qualities—though they may still be cold—add about 3/4 cup of your homemade tomato sauce. If you're out of that, Pomi, of scandalous Parmalat fame, still makes a more-than-passable tomato sauce that comes in an aseptic box.

Mix the sauce with the peas and "ham," let it bubble a bit, and set aside. Now the fun begins.

Start with the zucchini and, as with a *lasagne*, add a layer of each of the ingredients to the rice box in the *timballo* pan. If you have enough zucchini—meaning, if the kids haven't been through the kitchen, nabbing pieces—finish with a layer. Now take the remaining rice mixture and, using a piece of waxed paper, press the rice on top to connect with the rice on the sides and cover your box.

Bake at 350°F for 40 minutes. Cool for 5. Say a prayer and flip the *timballo* out onto a platter or large plate. Turning out the *timballo* is as thrilling as making castle turrets from sand and a bucket. When it comes out perfectly, it takes your breath away. And even if it cracks a little in the middle, you can push it together and dust it with finely chopped parsley.

April

Acceptance. Your child has choices. How can it be that your preferences are in the opposite order of the schools that he or she wants to attend? Don't you know what's best? No. As hard as it is to imagine, your child is the one who knows.

✓ To Do: *Write Your Own Obituary*

Does that scare you? I think it's scarier to think of what my loved ones might come up with. *She was really good at loading the dishwasher and worrying about her children.* See what I mean? How about the life that hasn't happened yet? *After years of happy motherhood, she returned to her life's passion of . . .* You fill in the rest from the abundant buffet that awaits you.

9 · Really, It's Called Mother's Day

MAY

RECIPE: *Spuntini*

No book on motherhood is complete without a birth story. Maybe our mothers shared the story of our birth with us, but we don't really have access to the experience of how we came into this world. We do, however, know how our own babies were born. I believe the circumstances under which our babies take their first breath are an important part of their story, a road map, a glimpse of what might lie ahead. I believe that the birth experience gives us, like our astrological natal chart, a little narrative of the themes our lives together will offer us.

For about six years in my thirties—the breeding years—I was either pregnant, postpartum, or almost pregnant. When I was having babies, I attracted friends in the same spot on their life path. We would share birth stories by way of an introduction. *This is who I am*, we would say.

"Hi, I'm Feather. I had a natural water birth at home with our extended family and our herd of goats present. It was beautiful.

Afterward, we all drank warm goat milk and the goats ate the placenta."

"Hi, I'm Sloan. I had a dramatic birth that required medical intervention. It's a modern-day miracle that either of us made it out alive. Between the two of us, we had half a heartbeat."

The story of Page's birth, which was the launch of my motherhood identity, so important to me at that time and place in my life, was somewhere in between Feather's and Sloan's. Well, not that much in between—it was closer to Sloan's, without the worry for our mortality.

Swept up in the natural-childbirth movement, I had planned that a little olive oil massaged on my pooty would be all the medicine I'd need. Childbirth classes described labor as work. Well, that's how it gets the name, right? A lot of work, with a lot of focus. I never shied away from work. And if I was under a deadline, I could focus like the best of them. For those of us with swollen bellies listening to the tales from the maternity ward, we couldn't help but judge what was a "good birth" and what was a "not-so-good birth." We had expectations. And we had confidence that we could control the experience. Confidence that we could control even the miracle of conception.

By September 1986, Jeff and I were ready to have a baby. We'd celebrated our first wedding anniversary on the first of that month, after a courtship and engagement totaling a respectable three and a half years. We'd been together for almost five years. We were ready. And since we are a couple of control-freak Scorpios, we wanted to have a Scorpio baby. We planned to conceive in February. I went off the Pill near the end of October in preparation, expecting that it would take at least three months for fertility to kick back in. In the meantime, we'd practice the time-honored and highly ineffective 1950s-high-school method of birth control. Yes, it's exactly what you think. *That* method.

I was pregnant before the Thanksgiving leftovers were gone.

"If you're sure of the date of your last period, which seems likely, considering the size of your uterus, your due date is . . . September the first," Dr. Yee told me as she heaved her big baby belly off the round stool. "Congratulations! And welcome to the club," she said on her way to see her next expectant patient and, by the looks of her, on her way to the delivery room.

So, we were going to have a Virgo on our second wedding anniversary. A Virgo? Weren't they supposed to be persnickety? Meticulous and orderly? Kinda uptight? Did we know any Virgos? Well, there was my loopy sister, Louie, and Jeff's even loopier grandmother Anna. Very loving women. Not known for their tidiness. They were Virgos. Hmm. A Virgo.

I know I was blessed to be spared the anxiety of trying to get pregnant and the heartbreak of infertility. More than one of my close girlfriends, after avoiding pregnancy for all of their adult lives, like the rest of us, found themselves waiting month after month for the stick to turn blue. I was as familiar with their menstrual cycles as they were. Happily, everybody in my closest circle of friends did eventually get pregnant. And (eventually) we all had healthy babies.

Jenna, Megan, and Loni were ahead of me. It went like this, respectively: natural birth at home with a doula and a cellist; emergency C-section at the hospital, absent husband, who passed out in the cab; scheduled C-section at the hospital after mani-pedi at the day spa. Moms and babies all fine. Those were the model birth experiences of my close friends. My mom's birth experiences, ranging from 1953 to 1969, were pretty much the same as Betty Draper's: shaves, enemas, episiotomies, gas, and Dad in the waiting room with cigars.

September 1 came and went. Time marched on for nineteen days after the due date, accompanied by nary a contraction. Doctor visits every three days, vital signs of Baby and me taken every other day. Blood pressure perfect, urine clear, baby heartbeat top percentile. This was just going to be my condition for the rest of my life. In another time, Mr. Doctor would have insisted on induction or some other invasive procedure. But Baby and Mommy-in-Waiting were fine, and unless Mommy-in-Waiting wanted to be induced, there was no medical emergency.

Finally, on Saturday night, I got menstrual cramps. Really bad menstrual cramps.

Page was born on a Monday evening twenty days after her due date. Her long and abundant hair, the condition of the white gooey stuff that covers babies, and the length of her nails confirmed that indeed she was a forty-three-week-year-old. During the two-day labor, she was never stressed out; her strong heart pulsed to a steady rhythm. The nurses changed shifts, went home and had a meal with their families, and came back to work, and still she hadn't arrived. I was comfortable. The epidural was amazing. I was pushing with each contraction, but Page wasn't budging. I don't know if she didn't want to leave me or if I didn't want to let her out into the world.

As the evening settled in on Monday, Dr. Yee came into my labor room again, this time wearing scrubs.

"I'll let you try to push for another hour, but that's it. I have an OR reserved. We could get you a baby right now."

"Let's get our baby."

After the birth—"It's a girl!"—the dreamy sleep of the recovery room, and the joyous energy of our loved ones welcoming her, Page and I were alone. I unswaddled my nine-pound, one-ounce baby and gazed upon her. I know that sounds like something Jane Austen might have described, but that would have been correct. For months you have this tadpole inside you, swimming around, but you don't know who it is, and then one day you feel it—a flutter—and the flutter grows into a connection. And you know. Your singular identity becomes the two of you.

Even back in 1987, it was popular (and easy) to find out the sex of the baby before the birth. You know, so the control freaks among us could pick the appropriate paint color for the nursery. Out of character for the two of us, we didn't want to know. We were fine with yellow and green. We both recognized that the surprise at the birth would be one of the best surprises life has to offer. But I knew. Not from ultrasound or genetic testing. I just knew. I knew I was going to have a daughter.

That first night Page and I were together in my hospital room, after the long, private moments of gazing, I swaddled her back into the tight flannel cocoon that newborns love and placed her in the bassinet beside me. I settled back into my bed. Before my eyes closed, I felt the first pang of missing her.

"What potent blood hath modest May."
—RALPH W. EMERSON

Of all the poems dedicated to the month of May and the promise of spring, this quote by Mr. Emerson gives me the best metaphor of motherhood. Is it any wonder that mothers are celebrated in this quiet month of the greatest possibility? What runs below the surface of our intense mothering, keenly felt during senior year, must be something biological. How else to explain our racing heart and upset stomach when our senior is out past curfew? There must be something in our "potent blood" that gives us the strength to refrain from calling the cops as we wait for the familiar car to roll down the driveway. There must be something coursing through our veins that is powerful enough to change our emotions from fear and irritation to joy in a heartbeat (when we hear the front door close from the inside, signaling that all is well), even if it is one thirty in the morning and we are wide awake. Turns out, there is.

Oxytocin, called the bonding hormone, is there for the taking. A natural Mother's Little Helper. When we womenfolk gather together, the biology of our closeness raises our individual oxytocin levels, and the whole group feels it. Comfort increases, trust blossoms, happiness grows. Our mothers and their mothers before them knew this. They spent hours in each other's kitchens, combining forces to make bread or gnocchi or tamales or *har gow*. Together they canned, they baked, they cleaned up. It was always about much more than the fruits of their labors. They needed to be with each other to naturally juice up their day.

When I think of the day-to-day of my mom and aunts, I remember them always being together. I'd come home from school, and Aunt Sue would be hanging freshly laundered curtains with my mom. Or if my mom wasn't at home, I was sure she was at a neighbor's house, having a midafternoon cup of coffee with a slice of gossip. They just dropped in on each other all the time, and we kids knew that our mom, or some mom, wasn't far away. It really was a village mentality.

That all changed by the time my own kids were in grade school. The mornings often felt like a fire drill. *Hurry, hurry, sling on the backpacks, don't forget the field trip permission slip, where's*

When we womenfolk gather together,
the biology of our closeness raises our
individual oxytocin levels, and the whole group
feels it. Comfort increases, trust blossoms,
happiness grows. Our mothers and their
mothers before them knew this.

your lunch? You left it on the counter? I'll fetch it, get in the car. . . .
And every day I'd see my fellow moms doing the same thing.
At the wheel of our SUVs, we'd give each other the morning
mom salute with *caffé latte* or Diet Coke in hand and head out to
carpe diem before the two thirty pickup. We were all doing the
same things—grocery shopping, errand running, laundry—but
we were caught up in the idea that we had only so much time to
"get it done" and that we were doing it alone.

No doubt we've come a long way, baby, but we may have
discarded something on our journey to performance equality,
something valuable and vital to our womanhood—our need to
be together. Oxytocin is not called "the love hormone" for nothing, and we're not called chicks because hens live a singular,
solitary lifestyle. *Cluck, cluck, cluck.* Feels so good to be with
your peeps!

As this "last" Mother's Day approaches, you need to take charge of the celebration. Because, love you as they do, your seniors are living the countdown to summer, and a "Happy Mother's Day, Mom" will be about all they can muster. Sure, they'll go along with family plans, but let's face it, girls, it will be more out of obligation than in the spirit of celebration.

It won't always be this way, so don't take it personally, and don't get all maudlin over memories of past Mother's Day gifts of handcrafted pencil holders and cards with little handprints. They're safely tucked away in your memory box. You did your October task, right? Good. It's spring now, and "modest May" is showing promise everywhere you look in the natural world. Daffodils and tulips are blooming after a long sleep. Another metaphor, Mom? This Mother's Day, you are going to blossom and honor all mothers in your own way.

Ditch the brunch. There should be a bumper sticker that says that. What woman wants to load up on a day's worth of calories before lunch? You graze along the line (getting your money's worth), and for the rest of the day, all you want to do is lie down. That's not much of a celebration. Oh, I was lured into that dumb-ass idea a couple of times. There was my mother-in-law to consider. But I had an epiphany many years ago. My toddler boys were fussing and knocking over orange-juice glasses, and my daughter was insisting upon sitting on my lap, while the "grown-ups" were enjoying their mimosas and eggs Benedict at the other end of the table. Enough said. This year, just have a quick cup of coffee with your brood and then get on with your day.

After the family coffee (and after you've opened your cards), plan to play some doubles tennis, jump on your bike, or go for a hike. Get outside and smell the beautiful world of May. Then,

There is a very contagious disease that goes
around in the month of May during senior year:
senioritis. You can remain vigilant in keeping
the virus at bay, but most likely, it will win. It's
not painful for your senior, and the virus does
run its course, though for you, Mom, senioritis
offers yet another opportunity to deal with the
prickly rash that comes at the intersection of
controlling and allowing.

full of energy, shower up, do your hair, curl your eyelashes, and
tie on your pretty apron. You are going to make a platter of
spuntini that you will take to the real party that you have planned
with your fellow senior-year moms.

While you're busy prepping for your celebration, your child will
be experiencing the first symptoms of a very contagious disease that goes around in the month of May during senior year:
senioritis. You can remain vigilant in keeping the virus at bay,
but most likely, it will win. It's not painful for your senior, and
the virus does run its course, though for you, Mom, senioritis

What's the thing that you are fighting about? Curfew? Calling in sick to school for a "mental health" day at the beach with some pals? Close your eyes and try to remember what it felt like to be on the edge of a new frontier. If you want to, you can enjoy this pregame party celebrating the beginning of their semiadult lives with them.

offers yet another opportunity to deal with the prickly rash that comes at the intersection of controlling and allowing.

I have watched dozens of girlfriends—particularly first-time senior-year moms—suffer greatly. I've tried to offer a little insight to my friends who were so miserable because the friction between their desires for their sons and their sons' ideas of what they liked to do was causing a huge, painful blister.

Around May of the senior year, your senior craves recognition from you, Mom. He wants you to acknowledge that he isn't a kid anymore. Aside from the fact that, of course, they still are kids, he's got a point. What's the thing that you are fighting about? Curfew? Calling in sick to school for a "mental health" day at the beach with some pals? Close your eyes and try to remember what it felt like to be on the edge of a new frontier. If you want to, you can enjoy this pregame party celebrating the beginning of their semiadult lives with them.

"I think I'm too old for a curfew," Banks told us over dinner one night at San Rafael Joe's. Like a Little Leaguer, he's still in his baseball pants, having just come off the field from another successful varsity game.

"Nothing good happens after eleven o'clock," Jeff said. He should know. According to the tales he and his friends tell about their high school years in San Francisco, the night wasn't over till the bars closed at one.

"Okay, no curfew," I said. I just threw it out there. Two heads snapped in my direction.

"Midnight," Jeff said. Agreed.

The next night, a Saturday, I heard the front door open past the time of Banks's old curfew of eleven o'clock. Past it by twenty minutes. They just want to feel the expansion. In a few short months, when they get home to their dorm room, hopefully from the library, their "curfew" will surely be out of your control. It doesn't have to be Christmas morning to open all the gifts. Give him one now. It will mean more.

For mothers who continue to uphold their role as keeper of the rules, the last few weeks of senior year will be defined by resistance. I felt bad for my mom friends who were so worried that Sonny might be up to "something" that they missed the sweet energy of watching their child step into his life. The seniors are ready for ownership. It doesn't matter what they do, as long as they know that "it" is on them. Choose to allow your senior to feel his independence. He's ready. Choose to allow the release of your responsibility for guiding his life. Choose to be happy. It's within your grasp.

♡ THE RECIPES

....

Spuntini: *Pollo con Salvia* (Chicken with Sage); *Radicchio Balsamico* (Sweet-and-Sour Radicchio with Prosciutto); *Melanzane Rolotini* (Grilled and Stuffed Eggplant)

Girls love the small-bite format. Little chunks of sage chicken, grilled eggplant rolled up and around fresh Italian parsley and goat cheese, and radicchio wrapped in prosciutto, dripping with a balsalmic reduction, are beautiful small-plate dishes that you can take to your hen party and share along with stories of motherhood joy, past and present.

♡ *Pollo con Salvia* (CHICKEN WITH SAGE)

....

WHAT YOU NEED

Perky breasts of free-range chicken

Flour

Olive oil

Fresh sage

Salt

Pepper

INSTRUCTIONS

Cut chicken into even chunks, a little bigger than 1-by-1-inch cubes. Dredge in flour or place in a paper bag and shake.

Heat some nice olive oil in a nonstick pan. (A few words about oil: The oil cooks the chicken, but it also imparts an essential flavor. I use extra virgin olive oil all the time, and, yes, I am familiar with the culinary dogma of this oil with this preparation. To weigh in on a discussion of correct oil uses and other snotty cooking-school topics, visit my blog: likeigivearatsas swhatyouthink.blogspot.com.)

Place many, many leaves of fresh sage in the hot oil. More than you think.

Just when the leaves start to change color, place the lightly floured chunks of chicken in the sizzle. Add salt and pepper to taste.

After about 3 minutes, flip the chicken, bringing most of the sage to the surface.

Salt and pepper again.

Cook another 3–4 minutes.

Serve on a warm platter.

♡ *Radicchio Balsamico* (Sweet-and-Sour Radicchio with Prosciutto)

....

What You Need

Radicchio

Nice olive oil

Balsamic vinegar

Thin slices of prosciutto

Pepper

Italian parsley

Instructions

Slice a head of radicchio into quarters, cutting north to south, not east to west. Cut out the white core, leaving a little behind to hold the leaves together. Depending on the size of the head, make eight or twelve wedges.

Heat olive oil in a nonstick pan and add the wedges, cut sides down.

After about 2 minutes, turn with tongs so the other cut side is on the heat. The purple edges should be brown.

After another 2 minutes or so, with the heat still up, splash with balsamic vinegar.

Turn off the flame and let mixture rest until you can handle the wedges without saying, "Ow, ow, ow!"

Wrap the slightly sweet and sticky wilted radicchio in thin slices of prosciutto.

Garnish with cracked black pepper and chopped Italian parsley.

♡ Melanzane Rolotini
(Grilled and Stuffed Eggplant)

....

What You Need

Eggplant

Coarse sea salt

Olive oil

4 ounces goat cheese

Italian parsley

1 sprig fresh lavender

Cracked black pepper

Instructions

Peel away wide ribbons of the beautiful purple skin of a robust eggplant.

Slice the exposed flesh lengthwise and lay the slices in a single row on a paper towel.

Salt generously and wait for the perspiration. Seriously, beads of eggplant sweat will form on the surface. It's like a miracle, a vegetable stigmata.

Cover the moist sliced eggplant with a fresh paper towel and absorb the salty excretions. Flip the slices over and salt again. Wait, watch, and absorb. Aggressively soak up the vegetable juice with the paper towel to draw out the moisture, the bitterness, and the salt.

Now place the limp and tender eggplant slices single file on a small platter (Italian ceramic if you have one) and drizzle beautiful olive oil on both sides. (You can layer the eggplant, oil, eggplant, oil—you get the picture.) Allow the slices to rest while you check the heat of your charcoal grill or grill pan.

In the meantime, mix goat cheese in a little bowl with some freshly chopped Italian parsley. I like to add a little fresh lavender to the mix. I know this sounds odd. Try it. But don't go overboard with the lavender. We don't want this to taste like soap. The trick is to add enough to mysteriously enhance the flavor but less than the quantity that would elicit the response "Oh, I can taste the lavender." You can use any soft cheese, but I say go for the goat.

After you've grilled the eggplant slices, let them cool a bit. On one end of the long slice of eggplant, place about 1 tablespoon of the cheese mixture and roll it up. Garnish with more fresh, chopped Italian (sometimes called flat-leaf) parsley and cracked pepper to taste.

May

You know that you will see her again. There will be winter holidays and summers, but most likely this will be the Last Mother's Day that you will have with all your chicks in one roost. You are clucking around like a fat hen. So if it's a day for you, do something for yourself.

✔ To Do: *Gather Some Girlfriends* *(Hopefully Mothers of Teens) and Plan a Party*
Tell your loved ones that you want homemade cards and cash. Gather the $$ and book a tarot-card reader, or a manicurist, or a plastic surgeon with syringes full of Botox, and have a chick party. Buy lots of booze to go with your *spuntini*—Italian girl

food—which pairs perfectly with the delicious buzz from the rising levels of "love hormone" you share with your fellow moms and all the mothers before us. Here's to you, Mom, the modest keeper of the potent blood.

10 · Mother-of-the-Graduate Dress

....

JUNE
RECIPE: *Orzo con i Pettini*

The funny thing about crossing the finish line is that you stand there panting for a little while, savoring your accomplishment only long enough for your brain to reset. Then you know what happens: Your thoughts turn to the next race. Senior year is all about getting the task done so you can move on to the next one. The milestones of completion pass in a blur because your focus is already on what lies ahead.

Graduation and commencement are separated by the thinnest of membranes. Endings and beginnings collide. On a sunny day in June, your child's moniker will change from senior to graduate. After he's opened money cards for a day or two, his designation will change once again, to incoming freshman, assigning him to the bottom of the ladder, though it's a better ladder than his high school one was. It reaches higher. It's the beginning of another race, and college freshman is the prize he's awarded for winning the last one. Finish high school, start college. That's been the plan this whole year, right?

But what do you do if this has been your plan and not his?

Finish high school, start college. That's been
the plan this whole year, right? But what do you
do if this has been your plan and not his?

"I think I want to take a year off," my youngest told me a few
days before graduation. This, of course, was a few months after
he had decided to attend a "sick" community college in "legit"
Santa Barbara. And many months after I had imagined my
house—and laundry room—finally empty of teen energy and
the daily detritus.

I gulped down a little chianti and replied, "What do you
mean?"—a stalling tactic I had learned from my teens.

"I'm just over it. I won't do well this year, because I don't want
to go to school. I took all those AP classes, and I'm over it. I just
want to chill."

I love teen-speak. It's great to be "over" something and to
"chill." We were on the same emotional page there. This was my
third go-round, and I was seeing the finish line of this stage of
motherhood. The idea of a graduated teen living at home with
us, just "chillaxing," gave me chills.

We hashed it out a little. I offered up Habitat for Humanity,
Forest Service, a program, a plan. That would be No, Bob. That
defeated the purpose of the year off. Getting a little part-time

job (big emphasis on the "little" and "part-time"), trick-riding his BMX bike under sketchy freeway overpasses, and hanging with the homies (the older boys who had already flunked out of school) was his idea of how he'd spend his time. By the end of that conversation, I was looking for some hash.

But instead of reaching for the pharmaceuticals, I did what any sensible mom would do. I took it to my book club.

"OMG!" was the first response from all five of the women with whom I had shared my life and my love of books for the past seventeen years.

"This will be a disaster if you don't have a plan." I feared that.

"How is Jeff [a traditional Italian hubby] taking this?" Poorly.

"In Israel, kids can't enroll in college right after high school." Encouraging.

"But without a plan . . . " Lots of head shaking and expressions of sympathy. Not. Good.

There was this consensus that I had to do something. That somehow this was a problem that needed *my* attention, a problem that I had to solve. I understood that position. It's the modus operandi in which we women have functioned since we became moms. When our children veer from the course, it's our job to steer them back down the acceptable path. We set the limits, teach of consequences, and, from our responsible leadership position, determine expectations. The sticky thing is that as we lay down the law about how another (our child) should live his life, we have to be the sheriff to enforce the rules and plans that we find agreeable. When there is a disagreement—"I have to be home at midnight? I'm the only senior in the county who has to be home at midnight!"—we offer an end point for our curfew authority. Eighteen years is just about enough time for

Eighteen years is just about enough time for us before we move on to another career.

us before we move on to another career. As for *my* role in law enforcement? I was over it!

Graduation day was approaching. Cards with metaphoric sentiments about setting sail on the sea of life were arriving from distant relatives. Little did they know, all my graduate planned to explore in the coming year were East Bay skate parks. I was inspired by the notion of standing on the shore, putting my toes in the water, and imagining a whole new chapter in the story of my life. I was preparing for my graduation, too. I was going to stop and savor the moment. And buy a new dress.

The dress I wore for Page's graduation is memorialized in photos. I don't think they make dresses like that anymore. I don't even know how I found it in 2005. A very unflattering shade of purple (purple!), with small white polka dots, it was full length, which for my stature isn't very long. It buttoned down the front, had short sleeves that hit on just the fattest part of my upper arm, and tied in the back like something from *Little House on the Prairie*. I never wear dresses like this. I curled my hair that day. I have straight hair. I don't know who I was trying to look like. It was a lost time. And you know what? I'm glad I have those pictures. How do we know where we are if we can't remember where we've been?

It used to mean something, the high school diploma. How did it get to be so worthless? Maybe we can blame the dummying down of the curricula, or the pressures of county and state governments to graduate the growing group of students who were already checked out by sophomore year, or the score-high-on-the-test structure that's insinuated itself into the American system of early primary education. The pressure to succeed is real enough, but those kids who feel it are the lucky ones—at least they're considered worth it. The kids who are behind or not striving for university are allowed to take the slacker track, and they graduate from high school with a diploma that will get them a job at the mall.

All of these trends have combined and reduced the pursuit of knowledge to just a means to an end. It's simply the thing your child has to do to get ahead. If he doesn't hit the gate running at the tender age of fourteen (i.e., the right high school, the service resume, the test scores), he'll be struggling just to catch up. No wonder our children feel pressure.

So I had a Goodbye Year that wasn't a Goodbye Year. I'd like to report that my son spent the year off reading Fitzgerald and Tolstoy, catching up on the classics he didn't have time to digest while he was running the race to nowhere. That he went to museums and volunteered at the homeless shelter. That the whole year was smooth sailing for all of us. But where would the growth opportunity have been in that scenario?

I'd taken yet another low-paying job in foodservice, this time at a bakery. I can't help myself. I love bread dough, puff pastry, *pâte à choux*, anything that conjures the alchemy of flour and butter, with or without yeast. I love the smell of it, the feel of the elastic in my hands, the layering of ingredients, the relationship the dough has with the day and with me, the baker. But it's hard work to show up and prepare quantities for the expectant public at five in the morning.

I'd come home from an eight-hour shift at one in the afternoon with a box of croissants, sticky buns, and cookies. My Gap Year Dude, Banks, would just be getting ready to start his day, hanging out in his boxers, under the blankets, on the couch with ESPN blaring on the television.

"Mom, what did you bring?" he'd ask me, now up from the couch and following me into the kitchen, with the blanket acting as a cape. I did bring the pastries home to treat him, and maybe to show off my skill and give him an example of my work ethic. I was proud of my touch with laminated dough. I had to get up at four thirty in the morning, when on some nights he was probably still up, playing beer pong with the homies! But even after all these years of parenting (growth whether you like it or not), I was still helpless against my need to please him. He was all I had left. Page and Ross were planted in grad school and college, and who knows where after that.

"Bones, this is the bomb bomb," he'd say, crunching and making a mess of croissant flakes on the counter. We'd laugh at the absurdity of his outfit, the "ridiculousness" of the pastries, and how this day, like so many others this month, the first of his gap year, was unfolding.

It was funny, but did it start to irritate me that I, Old Mom, had a job, ran a household, and found time to play piano at church while he, Young Able-Bodied Son, was just screwing off?

In a word, yes. It irritated me on several levels. But the mother guilt was first in line. I thought this was bad for him. And it was my fault that this mentally healthy, normal kid was not accomplishing, but rather doing next to nothing. He had worked with Jeff a little and did some landscaping for a friend. That reve-

This is the big challenge of the Goodbye Year.

What do you think about this life of motherhood?

What does it mean to be a mother? Who are you?

Question yourself: *Why do I think that?* As soon

as you open the dialogue with your higher self,

inviting the You of you in, you'll feel better.

You'll recognize her by that very fact.

nue and his graduation money kept him in gas and burgers for weeks. But this lifestyle couldn't go on. I had to do something. Bitch at him, I guess. Because if I didn't, he'd just be lounging, not demanding anything, having fun. That was bad, right? And then my question came to the rescue: *Why do I think that?*

This is the big challenge of the Goodbye Year. What do you think about this life of motherhood? What does it mean to be a mother? Who are you? Question yourself. We feel crappy because we hold beliefs that aren't working in our life, other than to do an excellent job of making us feel crappy. Question yourself: *Why do I think that?* As soon as you open the dialogue with your higher self, inviting the You of you in, you'll feel better. You'll recognize her by that very fact.

I listened to my better me, and, as with my approach to cooking, I felt my way into the situation: an aimless teen-man-boy-child living at home. We had a plan for deferment—he would go to college the following year—so I knew there would be movement next August, but that was thirteen months away.

"Mom, can I have five dollars for gas?" he asked me a few weeks after the money ran out of his slacker fund. Who could deny this boy? He's a cheerful cherub.

"No, Broke-Ass. I will not give you five dollars."

"Okay." We both laughed.

He got a job as a busboy. I provided shelter, food, cable television, and cell phone service. He spent the year doing exactly what he wanted to do. And so did I. He made a few rap/BMX videos. I got a couple of stories published. He contributed amusing tales of his day at the restaurant or at the skate park, and an infectious something else. Joy. A child's joy about the life he was living. Arrested development? Maybe. But the timeline was his, not mine, and it was lovely to behold my child taking the wheel of his boat and exploring, even if it was only in his own backyard.

♡ The Recipe

∙∙

Orzo con i Pettini
(Sea Scallops with Orzo and Early-Summer Peas)

The first time I made this dish, my inspiration came about from my freezer and pantry. I had a couple of leeks in the fridge, and I generally have butter and some form of cream cheese around. This recipe could have fit nicely into my series *Dalla Dispensa*—From the Pantry.

You may not think about going to your larder in June, with fresh produce and long days stretching before you, but this is a nice go-to dish that doesn't require a big shopping trip. The end of the school year is a busy time generally, and an extra-busy time during your Goodbye Year specifically. Your senior is busy with happy things, like last-of-everything parties, and you, Mom, are busy supporting all that. Though the early-summer markets in California are abundant, I found that during those last weeks of school, there were days when it was a comfort to skip the grocer entirely and pull something together at home.

What You Need

2 leeks

Olive oil

Butter

Salt

Pepper

1 bag frozen scallops

1 bag frozen peas

1 box orzo

About ⅓ cup mascarpone or American cream cheese

Instructions

If you have shied away from leeks because they look like *What? Do you use the bottom white part, the interior yellow-green? They're big and weird!*, put your fears to rest and jump in. Leeks are the butteriest member of the onion family.

Slice the root base off the bottom of the leek, and then split the shaft down the middle. Even if the interior looks clean, you need to rinse it under cold running water. When you ruffle the layers of leek, like a deck of cards bent in the center, you'll discover and loosen that one stubborn ring of sandy dirt.

Slice up the leeks, going from the whitest end to the yellow-green end. As you work your way up, discard the outer stalks and keep the tender yellow inside until you come to the part where it branches in two. You can save the outer, dark-green stalks and use them as a savory addition to chicken or vegetable stock.

Put your pile of white-to-yellow leek half moons into a large pan with some melted foamy butter and olive oil, and sauté over a medium flame with salt and pepper.

How much salt and pepper? This is what I do. I keep two ramekins next to my burners—one filled with coarse-ground kosher salt, and one filled with coarse-ground pepper. When I start a sauté, I melt the butter in the oil and look at the surface area. If I was going to have a bite of whatever I was cooking, I'd know how much salt (a little shake) and how much pepper (a pinch or a half grind) I'd want in that bite. Look at the volume of whatever it is you are cooking, and lay down the salt and pepper at the beginning. They are so humble that everybody takes them for granted—like a mom who's always there to add that important but unheralded (and certainly not sexy) element to all our dishes.

Add the frozen (seriously, still frozen) scallops and peas to the sizzle. They will release some water and start to make the "sauce." In the meantime, cook the orzo for about 8 minutes in a large pot of boiling water, generously salted.

Another few words about salt: I'm so grateful for it. I know that in earlier times, it was used like money. I get that. I use it liberally, especially in the water I use to boil pasta. How much? This is the kind of question that, when my cooking-class students asked it, I would answer with vague Italian sounds, a tilt of the head, and hand gestures. I didn't do this to be enigmatic or create some mystery around it; I really didn't know if I was adding 3 tablespoons or 1/4 cup.

Once the scallops and peas are soft, add the cheese to round out the savory mix. Save a cup or so of the orzo water. Drain the orzo and add it to the pan. Thin it out with some of the reserved pasta water. You can add another plop of butter to pull it together and serve in warm bowls.

"This never comes out like yours," Glenda told me as we enjoyed a late-afternoon St. Germain and soda at the counter of her beautiful California-Tuscan kitchen. She was making this dish, and the orzo were swimming in a lukewarm pool of watery cheese sauce.

"That's because Toni does that one extra thing that doesn't show up on the recipe cards," Tanya said, lifting her gorgeous, thick chestnut hair off her toned and tanned back. We shared a laugh, because I *was* a little guilty of that. I'm a good cook, but after a year of classes that were really fun and oversubscribed and gave me much joy, I had to come to one conclusion: I'm not a very good teacher. But thank God for my ladies. They didn't really seem to care.

June

Graduation. Seriously, wear something sexy. Dignified, elegant, but *sexy*. You're going to have to pose for lots of photos. Skinny tip: Stand with your arms stretched behind you as if you were standing between two linebackers who want to be included in the fun—shoulders down, chest out, spine straight. Everyone will say, "Did you lose weight?" and you did. You just shed a layer of ownership of your child. You love him still, but you are not responsible for his life anymore.

✓ To Do: *Plan an Overnight Getaway*

Or, if you can afford it, a couple of days. All this talk of your senior's upcoming launch will inspire you to step out in the world, too. Go visit that friend of yours who has been asking you to come see her for the past twenty years. Take a road trip, with or without a companion. It doesn't have to be a big Route 66 deal—just get out of town. A change of scenery sounds like a very simple thing, but isn't that the beauty of the simple things? Be present on your little journey, and you will nourish your soul.

11 · Nothing Says "It's Over" Like a Dead Dog

THE LAST SUMMER
RECIPE: *Glady Jusko's Sweet-Potato Soufflé*

"I'm going to get some new babies," I tell Page after a particularly testy exchange with her now thirteen- and fourteen-year-old brothers. All this bickering the boys do is exhausting. Exhausting for me. I think it's invigorating for them. They pick at each other and then call out, "Mom!" like I'm supposed to do something. I just want to smack them both. They needle each other. It starts out with "shut ups" and escalates with a shove or some physical altercation, and then I am compelled to put a temporary end to it with my yelling-mom routine. This is not who I am. Having to react to their struggles with each other demands something of me that I'm afraid I don't have. I can't figure this out. It sucks. For me. For them, it's over as quickly as it started, and they're out hopping curbs on their trick bikes while I'm left wondering how I manufactured this hell of motherhood. It's not the first time I remember that kittens are cute, but then they turn into what-have-you-done-for-me-lately cats.

"You're going to open a day care?" she asks with a head tilt that signifies incredulity. She is lighter now that graduation is over; her concerns are all fun ones: shopping for sheets and towels, making friends on Northwestern's in-house social network.

"More like a social club, a baby social club"—I'm speaking as I'm thinking—"but they'll have to be rich babies so I can be paid a lot. Rich Baby Social Club. That's it. That's the name of my new business."

"How many rich babies are you going to have?" She can't even say this with a straight face. It is pretty funny. I want to escape motherhood, but I'm looking for more babies.

"Two or three at a time. But there would be more babies in the membership. They just couldn't all come on the same day." I'm working out a business plan as I start mincing garlic and herbs for the tenderloin. The yearlong launch of my business idea La Cucina Semplice, teaching culinarily challenged ladies how to prepare simple Italian food, has evolved into a charitable operation. When my philanthropic friends ask me if I will donate a class to their worthy cause, I say, "Of course." So I create a lot of goodwill, and good things are done with the money, but, well, you can do the math.

That last summer the five of us were together, I thought a lot about babies. The three of them as babies. When you look into the face of a baby, it feels like you are looking at heaven. The energy that passes between you is so pure, and it flows in both directions. It's the purest love we ever feel. There's no history there, no intellectual connection. You just see them. Really see them. It feels like they "see" you, too. In their exquisite baby knowledge of the secrets of the Universe, they see the You of you. And through their eyes, you can see the You of you reflected, like they know everything about you, but all they see is the love. And

They are and always will be our babies.

This connection will never leave us.

The spiritual umbilical cord of our connection
isn't cut in the delivery room.

We will never emotionally leave them.

But we left our parents. Why did we think they
wouldn't leave us?

that experience of purity and divine connection imprints itself on us for the rest of our lives.

Sadly, the effortless flow of love that runs from mother to child back to mother stops flowing in our direction. Yes, yes, yes, they still love us (I guess), but that's life. Our children didn't know us as babies. Now, the person they see when they look upon our countenance during these teen years is someone who hassles them about the mess in their room, poor grades, chores left undone, curfews ignored. And even in the most troubled times, while we're navigating the unknown waters of this prickly parent-teen dynamic, we can access the echoes of the imprint that their essence has left on us. They are and always will be our babies. This connection will never leave us, moms. The spiritual umbilical cord of our connection isn't cut in the delivery room.

We will never emotionally leave them. But we left our parents. Why did we think they wouldn't leave us?

Their physical leave-taking is hard. Left behind is the hole of sound and smell. We are used to hearing their footfalls coming down the stairs, the slam of the side door, their one-sided cell phone conversations when they aren't aware of our presence. But you get used to it. There is the physical day-to-day of our lives that fills up the space. The emotional leave-taking is another thing.

Nothing says "it's over" like a dead dog. The summer before Page left for college, Indy, our dog, stopped eating. I'm thinking he's giving me shit because I bought some sale chow at Safeway. One day he's out walking with Marion the dog stealer, the next he's in repose on the porch, breathing hard, with an untouched bowl of kibble sitting next to his empty bowl of water.

Over the years he and I had come to an understanding. By the time my first Goodbye Year kicked into gear, I was totally tired of seeing his furry, lazy ass hanging out all day with that hangdog *When are you gonna walk me?* look on his face.

I'm like, *You're a dog. Go run after a squirrel. We live in paradise. Just watch out for the Sutton kid's speeding BMW on the Prospect loop.*

I think I was starting to push against the structures of Mommyland. Indy and I needed to design a new alliance. I'd watch my neighbor moms getting their shoulders pulled out of joint resisting the force of their canine's natural impulse to run free. For me, it felt like time to let go. I had just gotten so tired of thankless caregiving.

But what bothered me more than the lack of gratitude flowing in my direction was the constant resistance I got from Page's

> This whole model of Mom cajoling, enlightening, dishing out "for your own good" curfews and consequences, was wearing thin for me. I simply didn't believe in it anymore.

brothers, especially Ross. It was clear that her brothers' teen years wouldn't be as easy as Page's were. This whole model of Mom cajoling, enlightening, dishing out "for your own good" curfews and consequences, was wearing thin for me. I simply didn't believe in it anymore.

When the boys were little, it worked.

"No television tonight until your spelling words are done!" I'd declare. And, sure enough, they'd come through with an effort to do their work. But the great distinction between the grade-school years and the current middle-school and upcoming high-school years was this: My telling them to do stuff, and their arguing, resisting, and (under duress) doing it, wasn't all we shared. When they were little, there were bedtime stories and games and bike rides and cookie making and life. We were interconnected. But lately all we shared was accountability.

Now that the boys were feeling the independence that the teen years (and rising testosterone levels) bring, the days were starting to feel like one long battle. Ross had started lying to

> When they were little, there were bedtime
> stories and games and bike rides and cookie
> making and life. We were interconnected. But
> lately all we shared was accountability.

us about his whereabouts—stupid lies that in our small town would trip him up because I'd be innocently talking to another mom and the stories wouldn't match. Trust was eroding. My position of power was being questioned. He'd be starting high school in the fall. What would the next year bring?

And, being a mom, or maybe just being me, I was allowing my demons to tell me that everything that was going wrong with my fourteen-year-old was my fault. It is a terrible burden to feel that the troubles another is having are because of you. You feel that you should do something. *You're the mom. Do something!* Do what? Fight and bitch, bitch and fight. Was this all that was left of my joyful motherhood?

Maybe it was because Page seemed to have skipped the troubled teen years. She was never in my face with shrill exclamations of "I hate you!" (accounts of which I heard over cups of tea with distraught friends who had daughters of their own). She wasn't operating at cross-purposes with what a good mom wants for her child—a healthy lifestyle and strong academic direction.

I was allowing my demons to tell me that everything that was going wrong with my fourteen-year-old was my fault. It is a terrible burden to feel that the troubles another is having are because of you.

She was simply an easy child. A gift that seduced me into thinking that I was a good mom. It was her all along. She was already one foot out the door by the last summer, and frankly, I wanted to go with her.

So, Poor Indy or Lucky Indy, depending on your perspective, embodied the toll that my years of being responsible for everyone else and my fear of what the future held for me had taken on my identity as mother. I didn't like this new phase of mothering. I wasn't ready to give the boys the freedom they wanted—it was probably against the law—so, since I couldn't give up on my kids, I gave up on my dog.

"Indy, dude, you are no longer one more thing I have to be responsible for and guilty about. You want to be on your own? Clearly, you hate the leash. Wasn't that you who didn't come the other day when I called? Okay. Have at it. See you for dinner."

He'd scratch at the door, I'd let him out. The first couple of times, he slunk off looking over his shoulder like he was getting away with something. As if he could pull something over on me! But after a couple of days, he'd head out like all the husbands in the neighborhood, off to their normal jobs. But it wasn't normal. A dog walking alone—heavens to Murgatroid!

He was a free man during the day, but he needed to be home for dinner. And he got it. As I said, we had come to an understanding. He'd spend his day cruising the hood, going on walks with other dog-walkers, and just being a dog. I don't really know what the hell he did all day. This struck some of my neighbors as a form of neglect.

"Oh, hello," a voice panted into the kitchen phone. "I have your dog."

Then the helpful citizen with the busy schedule offered to sacrifice a few minutes to wait until I came round to fetch him. I did it a couple of times. It was the most expedient path. But once it became a regular occurrence with new neighbor Marion, it became clear to me that she was in the rescue business.

"Just let him go," I told her. "He'll find his way home."

"Oh, I could never do that! I'll walk him over," said the passive-aggressive, judgmental biatch—I mean, fellow mom. And that's how it started. Indy would head out to Marion's house, spend the day, walk around tethered to her extra leash, and be dropped off for dinner. One day I ran into them at the gas station. He's in the back of her SUV with her bling dog, Baxter, trying to act invisible. Like your teenager pretending that he doesn't know you when by chance you both attend the same event.

I've had dogs since I was a pup. I know dogs. Dogs are crazy about me because they sense a kindred spirit. I can tell you one thing: If they could talk, they'd say, "Let me take my chances." They're not stupid and they're not babies. They'd say, "Do you have any idea how irritating this name tag and license are, jingling around my neck like a high school girl's charm bracelet? You know, we're known for our excellent hearing. Day in and day out—not that I get out that much—I have to deal with chimes two inches from my sensitive ears."

I know, brother.

The week before I left for college, Bunky, our family mutt, knew something was up. I was spending more time in my room, deciding what I was going to take and what I was going to leave behind. He was hanging out a little closer to me.

"I'm going to college, Bunky."

"Am I coming?"

"Nope, just me," I said. He was doing that go-around-three-times move, like his ancient ancestors, before he settled into my covers. He crossed his paws and rested his alligator face on top of them.

"What are you going to do when I'm gone?" I asked him.

"Chase chickens, bark up the wrong trees, smell stuff," he said, lifting an ear. "And I still have the paper route."

"Who are you gonna sleep with?"

"Louie, probably," he said, before he remembered he had balls to lick. Bunky kept busy. I respected that about him.

The family dog is a marker of time, just like the marks on the kitchen wall that inch up every year showing your children's height. We got Indy when the kids weren't more than puppies themselves. On a sunny Sunday, the five of us climbed into the Trooper, drove to the shelter looking for a replacement cat, and came home with a eighty-five-pound sorta-kinda black Labrador. Oh, the walks and baths he would enjoy with the kids! How they loved their dog! How I loved the idea of the three kids and a

The family dog is a marker of time, just like the
marks on the kitchen wall that inch up every
year showing your children's height.

big, slobbering dog! It was during the acquisition phase of parenting. Life was huge and it was great. Of course, no surprise,
the kids lost interest, and I, like all the moms of all time, had to
take over his care.

I called his vet's office and told them about Indy's lack of appe-
tite. They said come right over.

"Hey, old boy," Dr. Opie said to Indy while rubbing the doggie
G-spots behind his ears.

"We'll do some tests. He's probably fine. I'll call you in a couple of hours," he said to me.

My phone rang just as I got home from the fifteen-minute
drive.

"You can come and get Indy. I've given him something to keep
him comfortable, but I wouldn't wait too long, not past Monday." It was Friday.

"Too long for what?"

"He's got cancer. Loaded. Stomach, liver. He's a stoic old boy,
but these things go fast."

What things go fast? Life?

By Sunday morning I couldn't stand it. I could tell he was in too much pain. And still, when I called him to get in the Trooper, he stood up, wagged his tail, and got in the back seat with the kids, just like he had ten years before. The five of us said goodbye to Indy in a white bead-board-covered room that looked a lot like our kitchen. His shoulders relaxed when Dr. Opie injected the first shot, and he smiled his doggie smile on top of a thick carpet embroidered with bones. And then he was gone.

Was I sad? Yes, intensely. More than that, I felt guilty for not having loved him enough, and this pain was my punishment. Was I entitled to my grief, since I clearly and visibly didn't give a rat's ass about his safety? I let him off the leash. But, wait a tick, wasn't freedom the real marker of love? Hey, I read *The Prophet* in high school. Jonathon Livingston Seagull would agree. Indy wasn't hit by a car or eaten by a bear. He died an old man's death, surrounded by his loved ones. He was ninety-one in people years. *He had a good life*, his obituary would say. Yet Indy's departure hung over our last August as a family like a ghost of what was and would never be again.

When people die in my world, there is usually a rather elaborate affair. Before the funeral, there are afternoon and evening viewings. I know some folks think it's kinda morbid to hang out with a dead body, but I think it helps to process the loss. When my loved ones die, we get busy picking out their outfit (if they haven't already made their choices known), the flowers, and the color of the nail polish to match the ensemble, figuring out where the out-of-town relatives will stay, and deciding what we'll eat. The busyness of the days and nights leading up to the burial helps with the pain of saying that final goodbye. And after the trip to the cemetery in my little hometown, there is a get-together with, of course, food. The church and neighbor ladies put on the feast and make their signature dishes.

We didn't have a funeral for Indy, though friends did stop by with their (live) dogs to offer comfort. Even Marion and Baxter. With a nod to "life goes on" and to the loving spirit of women and food, this month's recipe comes from Heilwood's own Glady Jusko. She made this dish for my mom's funeral luncheon, and Jeff couldn't get enough of it. Because of that, I make it every Thanksgiving as I quietly give thanks for all the women in my life, past and present, who have stood over a hot stove to give their loved ones a taste of the heaven that comes from their culinary magic.

♡ The Recipe

···

Glady Jusko's Sweet-Potato Soufflé

Typical of my hick-recipe collection, this dish is not a soufflé, nor does it contain any sweet potato. So what! It's still damn good. Indy would've lapped this up big-time.

What You Need

4 yams

¾ cup white sugar

½ cup plus 2 tablespoons butter

2 eggs, lightly whipped

2 teaspoons vanilla

¾ cup sweetened condensed milk

1 cup or more pecan halves

½ cup brown sugar

3 tablespoons flour

Instructions

Boil and mash the yams. Do not use sweet potatoes. Mix the yams with the white sugar, 2 tablespoons butter, eggs, vanilla, and condensed milk. Put the mix into a rectangular baking dish. Arrange the pecans in a pleasant pattern. Make a topping with the remaining 1/2 cup butter, brown sugar, and flour. Sprinkle over the pecan-covered yams. Bake at 350°F for 25–30 minutes.

The Last Summer

The days lollygag along. Your soon-to-be college freshman is home with you in the only home she has ever known. This is a pretty sweet time. The difference between the summer before senior year and this last summer can't be measured in calendar months.

✓ Last Summertime To-Do:
Paint Her Room a Color You Like

This will help with the cleanout and will give you a little break from the "I'm going to miss you so much" angst to imagine your new craft room, exercise spa, or art studio. Do not—I repeat, do *not*—make like Miss Havisham (and me the first time around!) and keep this former full-time bedroom as a shrine to your little baby. Your incoming college freshman is a big girl now, and so are you, and though she "technically" still lives with you, don't cling to that idea—it really is just a technicality.

Of course, they need to leave their Pee Wee Baseball trophies and cupcake dolls somewhere. That's why there are high shelves in the closet. This will be the room where they sleep when they come home for vacation. Changing the designation of the room will help all of you step into the rest of your lives. During this transition period, treat yourself to some girlfriend dates with those moms who have gone before you.

12 · The Dorm Drop-Off— Looks Like a Minimum-Security Prison but Costs Like the Ritz

Another September
RECIPE: *Bellini e Crostini*

It's nice to have friends at different stages of life, especially if they are a bit ahead of you. When you're suffering from sleep deprivation and trying to function in the depths of the physical exhaustion that toddler mothering brings, you catch a glimpse of your friend's life with school-age children and you think, *What a luxury to drop the kids off at eight thirty and have all day to myself.* When the search for a babysitter for date night becomes more trouble (and expense) than it's worth, you can't help but envy your friends who have a built-in babysitter in their oldest child, and you think, *How nice that will be to just be able to go out for a couple hours and have a little time to myself.* And when you're living through the last summer before college, you think, *Maybe this won't be so bad after all.*

Because during the last weeks of summer, it's time for your senior/graduate/incoming freshman to freak out. Your child is

---

When you're living through the last summer before college, you think, *Maybe this won't be so bad after all.* Because during the last weeks of summer, it's time for your senior/graduate/incoming freshman to freak out. Your child is getting a turbo-condensed version of what you have been processing for the last year. She has to individuate so she can leave you. Best advice: Be kind, and don't engage in her hysteria. This too shall pass.

---

getting a turbo-condensed version of what you have been processing for the last year. She has to individuate so she can leave you. Best advice: Be kind, and don't engage in her hysteria. This too shall pass.

Page was ahead of the move, of course. She started clearing out her room in preparation for dorm drop-off day by discarding blouses and sweaters she'd had since fifth grade.

"Great feng shui energy, releasing the old into the Universe," she told me playfully. She was echoing my words and making fun of another one of my woo-woo philosophies.

"I'm clearing out my stuff, too," I answered back. I tried to take her lead, but I was hopeless. When she wasn't looking, I'd remove items from her "to go" bag and stash them in my closets and drawers. I was making all her favorite foods in an attempt to get her to miss me before she left. We had a really nice summer.

I made an early-September date with my friend Julie, who was several years ahead of me on the motherhood journey.

"Bawled," she told me over our foamy cappuccinos. "Not a few tears, a couple of sobs. No, Jim *bawled* the whole way from Los Angeles to San Francisco. Even when we stopped for gas! I thought he might have a heart attack."

"I guess his heart was under attack, if you think about it," I said, as I tried to imagine the former college wrestler crying for six hours.

"Jim was inconsolable, though he waited until the campus was in the rearview mirror before he broke down. When he hugged Gwen goodbye, with his 'see you, little squirt,' I was feeling relief, mostly. Gwen had been such a pain all summer; if she wasn't being snarky with me, she was bickering with Jim about her freedom to come home at any hour of the night."

"What about you? Weren't you sad?"

"Sure, a little, but not like I was when we dropped Desmond off in Boston. Maybe once you've been through it with the first one . . . I don't know. It was different."

Hmm. So, the dorm drop-off can be a relief or a complete parent meltdown. Or a little of both. But it's a big something. It is a passage, a line in time that we cross and will always remember. Of all the mothers I talked with who had deposited their

The dorm drop-off can be a relief or a complete parent meltdown. Or a little of both. But it's a big something. It is a passage, a line in time that we cross and will always remember. There is joy in watching your children grow, but for them to do that, they have to leave you.

children on college campuses near and far, there were none who said, "Oh, I don't remember that day." Ha! Some moms likened it to the first day of kindergarten. That's a crying-mom day, too. In both cases, you're letting your child out into the world. There is joy in watching your children grow, but for them to do that, they have to leave you. I think what hurts so much is that we are reminded that our children were never ours in the first place. We use the possessive when we talk about them—*my* baby, *my* daughter, *my* son. On dorm drop-off day, we realize that it was only semantics.

Ross and I landed in North Carolina and drove three hours to rural northwestern Virginia because I wanted my middle child to see a little of the countryside that would be home to him for the next four years. He chose his small, private military college from a brochure, applied early decision, and signed on the dotted line, sight unseen. I snapped a photo of the "dorm" and sent it to my husband.

"It looks like a prison," he replied, "like something from a Nicolas Cage movie."

It did. I remembered thinking the same thing on the day four years earlier when we dropped Page off at her freshman dorm, though hers was more the minimum-security type where greedy stock traders go to repent. The campus was beautiful, resplendent with brick and ivy, but once we were inside the dorms, the rooms could have been cells. Page's roommate's mom and two aunties were already laying claim to the "better" side of her room, unfurling bedspreads and posters.

On dorm drop-off day, memories of the first to the last coalesce. Time stops being linear and instead stacks in a vertical experience. Your brain, or maybe it's your soul, expands, and you see and feel all of them at once. All the goodbyes resonate on the same plane. Past, present, and future collide. Chicago, Lexington, Santa Barbara are the same place in your memories. The place you said goodbye.

"Mommy, it's fine," my brilliant daughter whispered to me. My mama bear must have been showing. God, it's hard to let them fend for themselves.

"Mom, it's time to go," my confident, very shorthaired son told me. I was starting to take deep breaths. I could feel the juices of separation anxiety coursing through my veins.

"Good to go, Bones," my baby, my peanut, said to me, using the nickname he calls me when he wants to soften the blow of something I might not want to hear. When he's trying to lighten me up.

How did they all get so smart?

You will remember this day for every one of your little chicks

> You will remember this day for every one of your little chicks because it will bore a hole in your heart. But just look where you are compared with last September. Raise a glass of champagne to a job well done, and to the beginning of a beautiful, adult relationship with that lovely human being who just happens to be your child.

because it will bore a hole in your heart. What? This still hurts after all this self-help processing? Of course it does. You are and will always be a mother, and you wouldn't have it any other way. But just look where you are compared with last September. Raise a glass of champagne to a job well done, and to the beginning of a beautiful, adult relationship with that lovely human being who just happens to be your child.

Another September

Yesterday you couldn't remember the name of your neighbor's dog. "Must be the hormones," you said. But at the dorm drop-off, the complete script of a conversation you had with your son when he was five and lost his first tooth in the middle of the night comes rushing back to you.

"Something's a matter with my mouth," Ross lisped, his face like a full moon hovering above my head.

"What time is it?" I asked, which is something I always say when I am awakened. I think if a burglar broke in in the middle of the night, I'd ask him what time it was.

"Two three seven," he read from the digital clock. "Mommy, there's a hole in my mouth." He stuck the tip of his tongue through the space that the exit of one of his top front teeth had created. On the day I left him at college, he had a full set of teeth in his chiseled young-man jaw, but all I could see were the spaces left behind.

At the dorm drop-off, the weight of your toddler daughter's body, asleep on your shoulder at the fourth showing of *Beauty and the Beast*, will feel as palpable as a phantom limb when you hug her goodbye.

✓ To Do: *Pack Some Linen Hankies*

You can try to talk yourself out of the tears, but the tears will win. Give in to it. It's a big damn deal. There is a beautiful beginning here, and that alone is something to celebrate with tears of joy. But don't kid yourself—it's sad, too. How long it stays sad is up to you. You've done the work. The rewards are there.

✓ Second To Do: *Get Out of There Fast*

♡ The Recipes

....

Bellini e Crostini

You need a bellini, which is traditionally white-peach puree and prosecco, a sparkling white wine popular in Italy, especially Venice. In California, we enjoy an amazing season of white peaches, but that'll be long over by the time you dash out of the dorm. Still, it's not like autumn is a deadbeat. My seasonal take on this festive drink uses ripe pears, whose distinctive sweet grit pairs perfectly with the deep, metallic tang of liver on crostini.

Puree the first of the ripe pears, put a plop in a chilled champagne flute, top it off with prosecco, and sip in the maturity. Serve with crostini and savor the sophisticated flavor of liver and capers. Harvest is just beginning.

What You Need for the Crostini

½ pound chicken livers

1 tablespoon each olive oil, butter, bacon fat

Shallot, finely chopped

2 sprigs sage

Salt

Pepper

About 10 slices Italian or French bread

1 squirt lemon juice

Parmigiana

1 clove garlic

Capers

Italian (flat-leaf) parsley, finely chopped

Instructions

Clean the livers of any stringy membrane or veins. Chop roughly; set aside.

Heat the olive oil, butter, and bacon fat in a sauté pan over a medium flame. Add shallot and two sage sprigs. When the shallot is soft, remove the sage and discard. Add the liver. Salt and pepper to taste.

Meanwhile, toast the bread, preferably over hot coals or on a grill pan. Add a squirt of lemon and the cheese to the cooked livers. Mash with a fork or blend to a chunky paste.

Cut the garlic clove in half and swipe the bread with the cut side. Spread the liver mix equally over the toasts. Garnish with a few capers and parsley.

Epilogue: The Empty Nest

DECEMBER 2012

"What do you mean, she's not coming home for Christmas?" Banks asks me. He's got one final left, and then he'll make the trip home from Santa Barbara, where he is a sophomore at Santa Barbara Community College. "Christmas is family. You're supposed to be with your family on Christmas Eve and Christmas Day."

"Well, honey, it's different when you get older. Page is twenty-five. She and Eric are going to make some traditions of their own. It's okay. I'm sure she'll be home for other Christmases. Anyway, I can't wait to see you," I tell him. And because I'm still a mom, after all, I add, "Drive carefully."

It *is* okay. And I get it—though this will be the first Christmas without Page, and without Ross, for that matter. He's spending the holiday with some friends, and that's okay, too. I realize that as a mom, I used to want all the same things for my three children. But I know now that's impossible for many reasons, not least of which is the fact that there are three of them. They came one after another. The oldest gets to come home from college to the intact family with the younger siblings in high school or middle school. The baby has to deal with the fact that his older sibs may not be around. And maybe home isn't even the same place.

After Jeff and I sold Mescolanza, we used the proceeds to buy a neglected house in the neighborhood. We fixed it up and sold it. It was fun and profitable. We did it again and again. Designing the kitchen was a special treat for me. I loved thinking about the new mom who would cook dinners on the brand-new, beautiful stove, and imagining the love her culinary industry would bring to her family. But the economic downturn took its toll on us, as it did for so many other Americans. During Banks's Goodbye Year, we sold our home.

Moms were trending in 2012. We had our Previously Professional Working Mom-in-Chief and our Staying-at-Home-by-Choice Mom running for America's Top Mom. *Bringing Up Bébé*, Pamela Druckerman's examination of the French versus the American motherhood dynamic, got lots of panties in a bunch. The Mommy Wars featured in the blogosphere pitted one philosophy against another, which translated to mom against mom, woman against woman.

To add contrast to what comes after Dr. Sears's attachment model, Madeline Levine wrote in her second book on parenting (or what we should really be calling mothering), *Teach Your Children Well: Parenting for Authentic Success*, that failure is not a bad thing, and that the overscheduling of our children to help them succeed is actually hurting them. Levine considers that the more we do for our children, the worse they are for it. After the unimaginable tragedy in Newtown, Connecticut, Liza Long, a fellow mom, shared the pain of her motherhood in an essay titled "I Am Adam Lanza's Mother" in the *Huffington Post*. She got a million likes on Facebook and was skewered in the blogs for being a bad mom who couldn't control her son.

What is a mom supposed to do? Get a tattoo that says *It's All My Fault* and be done with it? Or we could do something else. Support each other. Quit judging. Let go of the defense. It's wonderful and it's agony being a mom. Hey, there's that growth opportunity again. At the end of the day, it's the same for all of us. We love our kids, and we are trying to do the best we can. Let's love each other, too. We can do this.

It's Christmas Eve. I have a bad cold and a big deadline. And the power is out.

"Was that thunder?" my city-born husband of twenty-seven years asks.

"No, that sounded like a tree coming down," his country wife replies.

Jeff sets up the generator so we have lights and refrigeration, but we still have to put the ham in the barbecue on low. Everything about this Christmas is crazy. The house doesn't even smell like Christmas.

Banks is visiting his girlfriend, who has electricity, and I sit down at the piano, start to play, and think of my mom. She was a Tiger Mom before her time, for me anyway. So much of what I am is because of her. If she hadn't grounded me for weeks when I got a B, I wouldn't have gotten a scholarship to attend college. If she hadn't called me in from hopscotch (every freaking day!), I wouldn't know how to play the piano. And if she hadn't been her, I wouldn't be me. How can I thank her for that?

There is a knock at the door, and I imagine it is a representative from PG&E to give us his condolences that the power won't be back on for quite a while. But it's not a stranger.

"Merry Christmas, Mommy," says Page, my little pigeon.

"She was getting sadder and sadder each day," says Eric, as he lugs in the luggage and the box of presents I mailed to them in San Diego.

I'm glad she was sad.

Goodness, what kind of mother am I? Just one who's happy that her children have wings, and happier still that sometimes they choose to fly home.

Acknowledgments

Of all the pages in this book, this one was the hardest to write. I started it a dozen times on paper and countless times in my head. My gratitude simply takes my breath away, and you know what happens when you're not breathing—you get kinda tense. The fear that I might forget to mention somebody froze me up. So here I am, mere hours before my final deadline, (naturally) not done. But, thank God, the Me of me stepped in and told me what to do: take the sage advice of the many amazing editors I have had the gift of working with. Stay on point. This isn't the Oscars.

I would like to thank Krista Lyons, Laura Mazer, and the entire team at Seal Press.

I would like to thank Annie Tucker for scaring me with her "pull the plug" speech, sticking with me when I wasn't coming through, and ultimately shaping the haphazard pages of my story into a book.

I would like to thank Book Passage, Linda Watanabe McFerrin and Left Coast Writers for providing a novice writer with a place to test out her prose. Out loud.

I would like to thank Danielle Svetcov for taking a chance on me.

I would like to thank my teachers and early readers Guy Biederman, Tom Jenks, Rosie Sorenson, and especially Rebecca Foust. Thanks also to my bestie Heidi Blair for cheering me on from a distance so I could get her done.

Thanks to my siblings, Scotty, Louie, and Nino, for encouraging me to write whatever I wanted to say.

Thanks to my husband, Jeff, and my three children, Page, Ross, and Banks. My love for all of you has made me, and continues to make me, a better person.

Finally, I would like to thank the Universe for delivering Brooke Warner into my life. At a reading almost seven years ago, she gave me her card and asked for my proposal, when the only proposal I knew about came with a diamond ring. I could have never done this without you, B. Much love.

About the Author

· ·

Toni Piccinini is an assistant editor at *Narrative* magazine. Her stories, essays, book reviews, and recipes have appeared in local and national publications. She owned a "Top 100" restaurant in San Francisco. She lives in Marin County with her husband and the occasional crowd of young people home for spring break.